TIERS OF BETRAYAL

"Loyalties Lost, Mental Depths, the Power of Redemption"

Eric Mamon

Printed in United States

Designed & Published by Hemingway Publishers

For more information about this book please visit our website at www.hemingwaypublishers.com.

Dedication

Helen Bowes. The females who have touched my life and the character I created who stole my heart, Sara.

About the Author

Eric Mamon is a first-time author at 54. He has been writing since his pre-teen years which proves it is never too late in life to start being a storyteller. Upcoming novels include Everyday a Birthday and Rise to the Abyss.

Contents

Chapter 1

"Sitting on the beach and my resting heart rate hasn't been this low in years" and... Post.

The July 4th Facebook entry of the day. A great run, beautiful day and finally able to relax for a few. This day has been an albatross that I continue to navigate year after year. Nearly 3 years after my divorce and I still struggle to this day. I spent 12 years of my life with a woman who was my love, my life, and I lost her. We met at an after-hours club on Independence Day. She turned my world around, brought me to this town and, in some ways, started this incredible career I have now. She is gone, but I still have the fruits. The betrayal of love is something I still have struggled with, yet I was fortunate to have this incredible experience of being in a place where I can heal and still grow. I am feeling better than I have in a very long time. Things are stable at the office; I can take a bit of a breath from what has been a tumultuous two-plus years as anyone can imagine. The company is staying afloat through the pandemic and after. Nearly reinventing our business model to an online platform, personally managing accounts saved not only my job but the jobs of 30 others in my employ. It was stressful, but I am proud of what me and Alec did. We worked hand in hand together. Alec Teachem has been my partner for the last twenty-plus years. More to the point, I have been his operations director and "right-hand man" through all the thick and thin that made Vivant one of the most successful small companies in the valley. Alec is the owner, and I am "technically" an employee, but I have never been treated as such. We are partners. Any and every decision made by this company for more than a decade has been collaborative. My...let's say our fingerprints together are on every aspect of the success that has put both our lives and future into an incredible place. He is the person I trust most in the world, and he has spent so much time mentoring and taking care of me through the hard times, my divorce, family deaths, etc. In all my circumstances, he is the person I turned to.

I always love to brag about Alec. He is smart, sharp, and can be a little awkward at times, yet positive to the core. He isn't someone who is built like an athlete but treats himself as such daily. There are so many features about him, how he carries himself as a husband of 30 plus years and father of 3 amazing girls, well, women now. He has a life I would dream of having. His confidence made him a man who I would refer to as a "force of nature." He can take over any room he stepped into. He taught me how to do the same. As I sit here on the beach looking out to the crowd gathered mid-day on this perfect Holiday, listening to my favorite 80's music, not having a care for at least the next 36 hours, I think of Alec and how he has put me into this position of comfort. There is no one I respect more in the world. I expect we have many more years to continue to work on the growth of the company. Through that, I can finally start to work on my own future plans.

I had spent the first 6 months of this year putting mechanisms in place to take control of my future, maybe even retire to do what I longed to do. Become a travel writer. Sounds a little cliché, I am sure, but to travel and see things. To have the ability to give perspective on those feelings, even mix in some food suggestions with that. I could be another Anthony Bourdain, sans the mental health struggles. Alec taught me how to "compartmentalize" emotions, slice them into manageable pieces, and swallow them whole. Those lessons have been very helpful in being able to just focus on the company growth. I do not let my personal crises get in the way. I refinanced my house, restructured my investments, calculated my retirement fund from the company, and came up with a date exactly 8 years from today. July 4th, Independence Day. Sounds odd, yet it fits me. Put a stake in the heart of my previous marriage and create a celebration day, instead of one of pain. It is funny how quickly these lazy days go by. Especially when not used to them. After a solid 7 hours on the beach, it was time to pack up and head back to my rental. Another quiet day tomorrow, and then back to the grind. I was so happy. I love my job. To have the peace of mind some would only dream of.

Chapter 2

Monday morning, and back at it. I pick up the phone and make my daily call.

"Alec, how's it going, bud?" I asked.

"Hey Aeron. Great! How was the shore trip?" he said enthusiastically.

"Wonderful, got a lot of rest and uh...well, it was much needed, thanks," I said.

"So, what's going on?" he brought it back in.

I knew we would be going into the weekly game plan. We have 20 facilities that we manage. All levels of needs that we both were in tune with. After all these years together, we could practically read each other's minds. We were so adept at knowing where we needed to be and where the team needed to focus that sometimes, we did not have to say much at all. Alec is a concise communicator. Succinct. Make it short, make it quick, and let's get going. He liked to read short emails, have short conversations, and expect solutions, not problems. I loved this about him. No B.S. It made it easy to know where you stood in any situation. These qualities sometimes left me in awe but never intimidated. I grew up with an overbearing father who used mind games to intimidate every aspect of my life and thoughts. Alec could be a man who would scream at me almost daily, yet for some reason, I never took it personally, was never daunted. Alec told me time and again, "I am not mad at you, just the situation." I believed him. I would not allow any other person to raise their voice to me, except him; it was something I could not explain, but it never affected me. We would get down to daily business, and reconvene on the phone at the end of the day. This was our ritual. What I looked forward to was the few minutes we had after debriefing on business to discuss life, sports, politics, and family. I was addicted to this routine. Being a man who thrived on regiment, this was a comfortable pair of jeans. Twenty years and two daily phone calls. Felt like I could never live without them. We created this amazing balance of business and friendship. I had never experienced this type of relationship with any other person. It was the greatest perk of the job. I have made many sacrifices over the years. I took 3 pay cuts, was being paid below market value for the job I did, missed vacations, holidays, and took a lot of stress that led to the demise of my marriage. I was OK with all of it. This company was something that seemed bigger than me. Plus, knowing that Alec had taken care of me for so many years, it was logical to think that this would be mine in some capacity in the future. All I needed to do was to stay the course and continue to do "Whatever it takes" for him, our clients, and employees.

Chapter 3

My days were never dictated by me. I had a framework for what needed to be done, but I was pulled constantly by people and outside sources. Only a few days off, a great holiday, and the stress was ratcheted up, per usual for me. Staffing issues are the bastion of my existence in this job. Relying on people is pretty much a losing proposition. I have learned that employees...people will always let you down. I had become highly conditioned to that and had contingencies for all of it. The problems I was facing were still lingering with the pandemic. All industries have suffered primarily in finding quality, reliable people to do the job. This day was no different. I had to cover a shift for an employee who had something "suddenly come up." He could not man his post that afternoon. So, as I had done hundreds of times over the years, I shifted my own priorities to make time to take care of this facility. My goal daily was to keep Alec and our client happy. While I was settling into the afternoon, double-checking closing procedures for this facility, my phone rang.

"Hey Alec, how's it going, bud?"

"Good, where are you at?" he asked.

"I am at the MJP site. Matt called off this afternoon, something personal he didn't want to talk about," I said.

"That's a bummer," he stated.

"Do you want me to call you after I leave here tonight?" I asked.

"No, I will come down there and we can catch up. There's something I want to talk to you about," he said.

"Is everything OK?" I stressed.

"Yeah, yeah, I actually got good news I want to tell you about," he excitedly uttered.

"OK, just get down here when you can. Can't wait to hear it."

I sat back in my desk chair, started to wonder. What news? Good news? Did we get another big client? Is a current client expanding our services? Is his oldest daughter getting married? I don't know, but I guess I will soon enough.

I started to pace the office a bit. It was a small office, not much room to move. I would walk 2-3 feet, then turn around and do the same. Maybe 20-30 times. Looked at the clock about 100 times. Tick, tick, tick. Why was I so worked up over this? Something didn't feel right in my head. I could not understand. Stress has a way of taking me over. I have a very complicated relationship with my rational and irrational mind. Rational is always right, but irrational moves the "goal post," so to speak. I spent over an hour of torture in my head before Alec arrived.

"Hey Aeron."

"Hi, Alec."

"Come in the office and sit down."

I saw a look on his face I had not seen before. This wasn't going to be one of our usual catching-up sessions. I felt it, yet I had no idea where this was going to go. I sat down to look intently. As he sat, I could feel his charisma come out. I have watched him over many years do presentations to potential clients, and it hit me that this wasn't going to be a conversation. It was more of a "pitch."

"I wanted to tell you, because you know how much you mean to me, and I wanted you to know before the rest of the company knows." He set it up.

"Yes," I responded sheepishly.

"You know Dan Rand of Comptor. He is buying Vivant."

I sat there as he said that. So much was going on in my head at 150 miles an hour. Dan was a guy who we had done business with over the years. I knew him, but not really "knew" him. Alec always dealt with the high-end business stuff. To say I was stunned was certainly an understatement. Not what I expected on this Tuesday afternoon. I could not respond accordingly, but Alec seemed to try and make everything seem OK.

"This is great for everyone. He has a much bigger company, lots of infrastructure, and more opportunities for everyone. And I am not going anywhere. I will still be on as VP of new contractual contacts, so we keep the continuity," he said confidently.

I sat there for half a minute, that seemed like a day and a half.

"What about me, Alec? Did you guys talk about me or my role? We have a lot of things in place that you and I worked out. Is that all OK, too?" I said with obvious concern in my voice.

"Oh yeah, don't worry about it. Dan will take care of you. We still have some things to work out, and you will be fine," he responded in a voice that seemed much less confident than when he gave me the 30-second "elevator pitch."

Now, the "things" that needed to be worked out were what I like to call "creative financing." Alec ran his business in a very unconventional way; a good portion of my salary fell into this. He paid me less money but made up for it with "perks." This was good for me and good for him as he got plenty of tax breaks by providing me with a retirement account, company car, and insurance expense account that covered my health insurance. There were "other" expenses he took care of as they came about. I knew Alec did things a little differently and I was a full beneficiary of all of it. I am smart enough to know that with this meeting, these "perks" were at best, up in the air. At that time, I didn't even speak about my company position. With my head spinning, losing my title was not in my present sense. He could feel a little angst in me and wrapped things up quickly, shook my hand to leave, and said, "We will talk more." He walked out of the office to leave me in a practical silhouette of my anxiety hanging over.

Chapter 4

I began to process this as I was making my way home. I found that I was struggling with 3 buckets of emotion.

Left bucket: I was happy for Alec and his family that they will now be able to fulfill their dreams to be able to enjoy the fruits of 35 years of labor in building Vivant.

Middle bucket: I have lost my confidant, mentor, and one of my best friends. The person I talk to twice a day, every day is more than likely gone. The man who has given me all the confidence to do the job I have done for him for nearly 20 years.

Right bucket: my job and future may be in complete limbo. Is what I do worthy? Necessary? Profitable? Will my new boss feel about me the same way Alec does? I have no idea. I can see many horrible nights to come until this is figured out. I am going to have to weave everything I have learned over the last 20 years to make this work. I have the skill set, savvy, and experience to be able to work through it. I can only hope. Dan did reach out to me today to give me a vote of confidence, but I know that the emotion, and the care that Alec put into me will be gone soon as I will be starting over. Close to my mid 50's, I feel I am at square one. It feels exhausting. What is my future now? Why don't I have an answer to that question? I have to say that when Alec sat me down yesterday afternoon and told me the plan, it took me back to 3 years earlier, probably the worst day of my life. That was my anxiety in bed at 3:30 AM.

My ex-wife had this similar "blindsiding" conversation with me on a Tuesday after the Labor Day Holiday. She had a look on her face I had never seen before. "Did something happen at work today? Are you OK?" I asked. I was frightened, but never expected what came out of her mouth the next second. "I am not happy; we need to talk to someone." I felt my knees give out. The love of my life, everything I worked for, my soulmate, was not happy? That minute was the beginning of the end, and my helpless emotions proceeded to live through two years of worthless marriage counseling bullshit exercises. I watched as my life was torn down brick by brick. This situation with Alec couldn't be the same thing. This was work. I am one of the most experienced people doing the job I do in the industry. Surely, Dan would welcome me on his team. I could seamlessly move into the same role. I know Alec has put things in place to ensure I will be taken care of. I cannot compare any of this to my marriage. She wanted out and could not get rid of me fast enough. Alec is my "brother." It is different. Totally different.

The mad dash began the next day. A hastily called meeting with the entire Vivant team to make the announcement. I had not slept the night before. I was still in this whirlwind of "What the hell just happened?!?" Being a good soldier, yet shell-shocked, I just followed along through the day with what Alec was looking for from me. "Stay positive, this is great for everyone, you will see," Alec was ever convincing. "They are really looking forward to working with you."

As the morning went along, I received a text from Dan; I am honored to finally have an opportunity to work with you. I responded kindly, although I didn't mean any of it. What is going on? I have barely been able to get my breath from it all. Less than 18 hours and I am seeing my career pass before my eyes. Got through the morning and waited on a "Zoom" call in the early afternoon for Alec to announce the news. Thirty employees, Dan Rand, and his wife. Laura Staley, Comptor Operations Director, whom I had known for nearly a decade. There was also a young woman who I didn't recognize. This person was announced as Comptor, Inc.'s Chief of Staff, Ali Howard. "Chief of Staff?? Where the hell are we in, the West Wing?" I thought silently. "Look at this girl, my gawd, she doesn't look any older than 25. I had interns who looked older than this." Again, my thoughts were racing. For the next 30 minutes, I could barely comprehend. I watched as stunned faces listened to company propaganda that was being spewed on both sides. Alec was speaking like I had never heard him before. This was a man so passionate about his company. All the years he put in to save it, build it, make it the best in the industry. I served him with that same passion. I was hearing a man who seemed relieved that he was letting it all go. Dan Rand gave an awkward, unmoving speech. I had known for years that Dan was not a polished speaker. He tended to trip over himself often. Deferred public speaking to others. Especially with the contracts we collaborated with him, Alec handled all the public relations. This first meeting crystalized, or so I thought, of his lack of engagement on a public stage. I would soon learn a lot more about this "autistic savant." No questions were allowed to be asked. Things would be staying "status quo" through the transition. During the last few minutes of the meeting, I became fixated on Ali. "Chief of Staff?" How old...maybe

26-27. "She looks miserable on this call," her sourpuss face and pursed lips carried a real "mean girls" sense about her. All I knew after that meeting was that I needed to take some time off to process. I had a call with Alec later that afternoon and did not even address the day's events.

"I need to take the rest of the week off, Alec."

"Are you OK, bud?"

"No, Alec, I am not, I just need a little time to take all of this in."

"Aeron, I am worried about you. Alright, do whatever you need, and oh yeah, we are out of our office in 2 weeks, so when you come back, we will get together and start packing everything up."

The office, this little 200x200 oversized closet that we used for almost 15 years as our meeting place, where all decisions for our success were made was going to be gone too. I just had to get out of this space for a while.

Chapter 5

Four days off and three "status quo" days of work before I made first contact with my counterpart. The time off did not help; I was no better emotionally than the week before. Laura Staley was a manager for me starting almost 12 years ago, lasting about six years in total. She was attractive, although always a bit disheveled. She appeared to have multiple things going on, yet forgot that she had to dress herself and comb her hair in the morning. Her hair was something I could never understand. It was a cross between Rod Stewart 1978 and Melissa Etheridge 1998. Her husband seemed to have the same stylist. In the multiple times I had met him, he had a definite look of being "Hot Rod" in the "Maggie May" grainy concert video from the early 70's. She was an organized, focused, extremely IT-savvy person. Not much for people skills, but her face was just trusting enough that no one looked at her with a cross eye. She wore a mismatched shirt and pants. Something you would not expect from a female in a professional work environment. This first meeting was when I started to feel that my job, as I knew it all these years, was going to change. She went straight into "twenty questions" mode about my job, responsibilities, and all nuances—a nice way to break the ice. I was taken aback, considering I was her "boss" for enough years that she should have already had a good idea of what I did. What stood out for me initially was just the utter inexperience she had in dealing with the basic aspects of her job to try to nail down mine. I knew that Alec had helped her get a job with Dan Rand a few years earlier as an administrative type of person. Her skills would have impressed anyone working in a clerical type setting. I figured she shined as a paper pusher. Leadership, the aspects of client relations, I did not see any of that, out of the gate. I needed to get a better handle on her, but I also had to prepare that she was going to become my daily contact. The days of speaking to Alec twice a day were now over.

I left the meeting and only wanted to call Alec to drill him about this disjointed conversation I had with this "former employee" of ours. I refrained. I wanted to respect his space. To understand that he was now "retired" with a figurehead title of "VP of new contractual contacts" (insert raspberry here). Over the next few days, we had a few uncomfortable phone calls. It was not the same anymore. I watched earlier in the week as he scrambled to set up client consultations with all the accounts we worked on together for many years. He went full court press doing the "sell job" alongside the new owner. I am sure those meetings were just as clumsy as ours from the previous week. I was embarrassed for them. I made a point that day that I would at least try and open my mind to this "new normal." I still believed in my ability, experience, and clout internally, along with our clients, that I would be able to navigate this. I was prepared to find what that new place would look like. I would give Alec the benefit of the doubt. I still believed he would look out for me in the end. I mean, come on, we had been "brothers" for nearly two decades. All of this would settle down; I could still keep my plans and do my job. My experience would keep the cache that I had worked for and earned.

As I try to convince myself and possibly pump up my own ego, I naturally go back to my marriage. We went through two stints of counseling. The first was "successful," well, at least in my mind. It felt like I dodged a bullet. We went back to our everyday life, normal sex, normal everything. She was her old self for about six months, and then I got the penultimate blow around the Holidays, "I need to talk to someone," she said. This was different than we, so I was not as horrified as the first "talk to someone." That all changed a few months later while vacuuming the house and stumbling on the Life is Good, Why You Should Leave Anyway book half read on the floor under the bed. That turned out to be the "Oh Shit" moment. Everything after that was downhill.

I did not know my ex-wife's therapist, but I had a pretty good feeling the woman was a man-hating feminazi. She was never the same. Within a year, our life together was over. I needed to be cautious with the power of positivity. I had been through the wringer before. I did believe I had a little more control this time around. All I had to do was produce results, nothing about emotion. This is a job, not a relationship. Plus, Alec is a dude. Dudes look out for each other. No female complications, sex, or bringing up the past. The issues that never mattered. All Alec had to do was look out for me, be fair, leverage our multi-years together with a new owner who should relish wanting to work with me. I know I still have so much to give.

Chapter 6

Alec and I met for the first time almost 20 years earlier, mostly in passing for the first six months. I was hired by his partner at the time. A man who was, quite simply, evil. An egomaniacal prick who drew pleasure from torturing people. No matter who you were in the company at that point, everyone had a "Sam" story. Samuel Steven Staab. He liked to use his middle name when introducing himself to clients. It was quite nauseating. Sam carried himself like a CEO. He was "The Man" and made a point that everyone knew it. The Khaki suit, plastic smile, and fake persona just oozed from him. I hated him during my interview, but I was driven. I wanted to take my career to another level; he figured it to be a calculated risk I was willing to dive headfirst into. My days working under him were a mix of torture, suffering, and punishment. I certainly never felt worthy. Great for anyone in my life at that time. I worked late nights and weekends and arrived before anyone else. It was a pattern that I mastered early on, but working for Sam Staab was more about survival than anything that could build a career. I spent time with employees under me who spoke of "That Asshole" all the time. Sam tended to forget that employees must be paid or have health insurance premiums covered. He docked an employee for missing a day because she had to take her sick daughter to the ER—a real quality human being.

On Thursdays, we had a companywide manager's meeting; this is when I first had a chance to get to know Alec a little. He was the opposite of Sam. Engaging, charismatic, down to earth. He was like no one I had ever met in his position before. Alec was partners with Sam. From the first day, I could not understand how these two most diverse personalities ended up as business partners. Alec had a breadth of knowledge of sports, music, and things entirely non-conventional for business. He made you feel at ease in his presence. I gravitated to that quickly. I was still relatively new to the industry—only a year plus overall in this type of position. I was looking for a mentor or just maybe anyone I could connect with. As a Type B person, being driven is not something that came easily to me. I was good at being disciplined, regimented, and consistent. Security blankets, so to speak. Alec had a personality that seemed to mesh with me, although I was cautious to just focus on my job. We would talk for 10-15 minutes, and away we would go to our responsibilities. I knew early on I wanted to get to know him better. I liked him from the beginning. It would be a while before that would happen. Right now, I was just trying to keep my head above the fray, hoping that Samuel Steven Staab wouldn't have me for his lunch anytime soon.

Chapter 7

Betrayal. This is all I am thinking about as I try to control a panic attack. The last ten days have crystallized what that word means in my life. As of this morning, I officially no longer work for Alec. So many years spin, like riding in a Camaro on a highway and seeing mile after mile roll right by at 80 miles an hour. I am in this "Fake it until you make it" stage, yet I do not understand what that exactly means. No one has spoken to me. The status quo, the new normal. What the hell is that anyway? Did Alec hang me out to dry as he rides off into the sunset? Am I left to figure out if I have what it takes to continue with this company in this environment? Why hasn't anyone spoken to me? I am frustrated, or am I? Uncertainty is the problem. Why was I left out of all of this? I feel overcome by emotions that should not be happening. This is starting to add to the long list of people who have completely disregarded me despite my loyalty, sacrifice, and decisions for them and not myself. I just spent the last six months creating a 10-year plan to complete my career to ride off into the sunset. That is now up in smoke. This occurred for a reason; I must believe that.

Is it to stay with Comptor? I will work the "Chameleon" as long as I can. That is what I am good at. The "Chameleon" changing colors to fit the surroundings. This old friend has pushed me along for so many years. I have never felt like someone who has ever had a great deal of talent at anything. My talent is taking advantage of the opportunities that have been presented to me. This one may be a bit different. I do not initially feel I have any prospects to take advantage of. I have gotten no signs, doors open, or windows to something on the periphery. I have never felt this way before. I have work to do to figure this out. Ali Howard will be the next step.

Back to Betrayal. That is the crux of the real issue of what defines my life. Everyone I ever trusted and loved has turned their back on me. In recent times, I lost my best friend of 25 years. Clint and I met while bagging groceries in a small store in Phoenix. A guy with James Dean looks, talent, and personality who would take over the world. I always gravitated to this type of person. Someone who I looked at was better than me in some way, anyway. Clint had artistic talent. He was touched by the hand of God. He could draw, sculpt, and have any woman in his bed within 3 hours. I became obsessed with him at 18 years old, and that carried me into my early 40's. He taught me how to dress and act around women, and he even experimented on me with his intimacy issues. He was the only man I ever kissed, and I never questioned when he brought it up. It was Clint's exploration. I was just on the journey with him, as with every relationship in my life. It took its course to end on his wedding day. I was supposed to be his best man, and he was mine. The day he took his bride, I stood in a crowd of 100 as someone else took a spot that should have been mine. I did not know until that moment. I stared him down. He gazed at me, then looked away. I walked out, never to see him again. All those years melted away. I sobbed and accepted.

My wife and the one man I believed was my faithful friend for life and would look out for me—still so much to process and no direction anywhere in sight. Now I think of why Alec would do this to me. He knows my life struggles. The pain and ache that has engulfed me for so long. I told him everything; I ripped my insides open for him to see me bleed. Very few people I have been able to open my heart to over the years. This all cannot be real. I am exaggerating all of this. I am just paranoid. Everything will work out. My basic instinct is always to think of the worst. Therapy almost a decade ago did only so much. It didn't help my marriage. I can only long for this situation to all work out. Alec loves me, and he will make all this right.

Chapter 8

As strange as they are, I have begun to get settled into my daily routines with Laura Staley. She is very bright, but her actions in business seem to get her nowhere. I think of her as a "hamster." This poor little animal who gets in that wheel and goes goes and goes, never to get anywhere. She communicates from both sides of her mouth. Her filter is non-existent. I get feedback from employees who continually check in on each other. "Did you hear what Laura said about you?" "She is talking shit about Jeff." "She is not a fan of Sharon." Then I get the gut punch, "Hey, are you going to do anything about this." That is my trouble. I cannot do anything because I have no power, or at least I don't think I do. Nearly a month in, and still, no one has spoken to me except Laura, who just babbles on yet never gets us anywhere - just like a hamster.

It is Thursday, and I have my first "official" meeting with Chief of Staff Ali Howard. Alec had informed me that she is bright, got her stuff together, and is "hot." I didn't need to hear the third part of that. I couldn't care less what she looks like. She is one of the people who now has my job in her hands. I need to figure out what I am dealing with. Everything this company does is virtual, and to say I am "virtually fatigued" is an understatement. I am wired for connection - physical connection. I love to sit face-to-face with someone to have a conversation. The

Pandemic killed that. I am now preparing for meetings with a president who lives in Georgia, a Human Resources manager who lives in North Carolina, a Chief of Staff who lives in Minnesota, and an operations director, the "hamster," who is local but hardly a face-to-face person.

First impression: Ali is sitting in her living room, stuffing her face with something, and it looks like she just returned from Target. She is wearing a sloppy blue blouse that hardly fits her. I am sure she can look better than this. That shirt does her no favors.

"I apologize; I am running a little late and haven't had lunch yet." She states.

It is 3:30 in the afternoon. We are closer to dinner than lunch. Considering this was the first time we met one-on-one, I got the initial intuition that she was not looking to score any points with me. She cluelessly goes through aspects of my previous job and makes a statement.

"Aeron Harmon, Laura says good things about you." She should, she worked for me for six years, I thought.

"Thanks, that's nice. She is a good colleague." I respond.

Ali has a horrible delivery when trying to converse. I would say wooden, but that would be a compliment. She then went through the plans for the company's conversion to a Google platform and all the other performance platforms they use. Plan A for this, Plan B for that, Plan C for something else. Every facet of our 35-minute meeting was forced. I felt she could not get off the call fast enough. All I can think of is this woman reminds me of the last two interns who worked with us. Awkward, smart, maybe. Millennial, very millennial. Entitled and coddled, she thinks she is the smartest person in the room. She is the "Intern." I just felt thunderstruck that my new boss is a glorified intern. As I sat at my computer after the meeting in silence, I recognized that the two people I will be working most intimately with in my job are a "hamster" and an "intern," and I still don't know where the hell I stand in this mix.

I got off the call and remembered a few moments later that Alec needed me to help him finish moving our old office. I left my home office and headed to the location we had moved into together so many years earlier. When I arrived, the room was nearly empty. Just a few meaningless filing cabinets, boxes, the stuff I had accumulated over the years. There were still two chairs in the room, and I sat in one. Alec decided to sit in the other.

"Alec, what the hell is going on? These people are turning the company upside down. They are adding platforms no one understands, screwing up email accounts, and Laura is talking shit about a multitude of our employees. You need to talk to Dan about this. It has barely been a month; why do they need to change everything so quickly?"

"Don't worry about this so much. Dan and his team know what they are doing."

"You keep telling me that. No, they don't!! What is my position, Alec? No one, not even you, has explained that to me yet."

"Relax; I will talk to Dan and let him know your concerns."

"What is happening here, Alec? I have been losing sleep for weeks now. No one prepared me for any of this. I am the one most affected by this merger, and no one seems to care."

"Aeron, it will be fine, trust me, it will work out. They know how important you are to all of this. Just load up your car and get home. I am sure it has been a long day for you."

I loaded my car with the remaining stuff from our office. I returned, stared at the hollow space, reminisced for a moment, and left. I would never return to this building again.

I drove home with the radio off. The uncertain feeling continues to weigh on me. Why has no one sat down and talked to me yet? This was taking the most toll on me. It seemed that no one cared. I took a few deep breaths and let it pass. I would begin dealing with a series of meetings starting tomorrow called the "Get to Know Dan" series. This is our new President officially introducing himself to the team. I can only imagine how that is going to go.

Chapter 9

As I sipped my coffee the next morning, I could not help but think about this "Get to Know Dan" thing. It was Friday, and most of us had pretty much checked out for the week. Being in the position I "used" to be in, I was always cognizant of every aspect of the company. Not only what I did but what the optics looked like to everyone on our team. It did not seem to be the right time or day for Dan to call these sorts of meetings. He scheduled 3 of these sessions to give all Vivant employees the flexibility to participate when it worked best with their schedules. Laura had asked me to be a part of all three meetings to show strength. Considering that these employees had answered to me all these years, it was critically important for me to be on all the calls. I was over a month in and still have not had any face-to-face with Dan, so this first "team" meeting would be the first chance I would get to see him. The connection with him on a leadership level. This meeting was going to be Virtual. I learned quickly that the first of the many awkward issues of 'him,' let's say in a nice way, "car crash." 2:30 came, and away we went.

The first call was given to 12 of our employees, me, Laura, and Ali. Dan came onto the screen. The President of his company, Comptor. T-shirt, sunglasses on head, severe Wi-Fi issues. I tend to wear my emotions, face, and body language on my sleeve, so the bug-eyed look on my face was certainly prevalent. I was squirming in my seat while still trying to look professional. It was important that I exude a level of "I am still your leader" to all my employees. Dan fumbled; Laura and Ali were slopping up, trying to provide suggestions for the issues he was having on the call. It was awkward, weird, and pretty much par for the course over the last four weeks. After a few minutes, the main event proceeded.

"Hi, as you know, I am Dan Rand, the President, and I am here to talk a little about myself today. I am not comfortable putting myself out there like this. Alec is much better than me at this."

He spent the first 2-3 minutes trying to get comfortable in his skin, talking to all of us. It really didn't work. I will cut Dan some slack. Alec was what he liked to call himself. A "hambone." Someone who thrives on performing in front of people. If anyone knows the definition of "hambone," it is not the most comfortable phrase to use, especially in business circles. Alec was a performer and used the term often. I had seen him in dozens of venues; the man knew how to command an audience. That was not Dan Rand. After a few deep breaths, we were back on track. This was painful for me, and we hadn't even started with the meat and potatoes.

"I want you all to get to know me; I am going to show you my belly button today."

Wait...what did he just say? "Show me his belly button????" Did he really say that? I go back to a classic movie of youth to refer to what is happening at that moment, "We are not in Kansas anymore." I sat in awe as this man, an Ivy League graduate owner of a multi-million-dollar company, made a complete and utter fool of himself over 45 minutes, bumbling and stumbling over the English language. He continued to dance on my grave as a leader in this company, as well. "Belly button" exposed. I was waiting for him to ask for a lifeline. I would have gladly provided it for him, but as I was to find out, I was invisible.

The breathtaking performance mercifully ended. We all dropped off the video call; I sat at my computer, in a somewhat catatonic state, trying to register what I had witnessed. I can only imagine him talking to his wife or Laura and Ali about his performance. As I was thinking, my phone went off. Text from Dan. "So, how do you think I did?" I sat staring for a moment. Honesty or good soldier? Ugh...I chose a good soldier: "Dan, I know the employees, and all they want is someone who is authentic, and you showed them that today." I hated the second I sent it. My heart told me to say. "You are a joke of epic proportions, and I cannot believe Alec sold this company to you, Moron." Survival causes us to sell our souls sometimes. I was in no place to say anything to folks I hardly knew or understood. Dan responded to my text, "Thanks, I thought it went OK, too." God help me.

I had to suffer through two more of these, and none were better. I didn't get a text from him after the second or third, but Laura and Ali seemed pleased. The "hamster" and the "intern" were on board, and as each day passed, I was more convinced that these were Dan's inner circle; I wasn't. That would become a problem, I figured. I still felt like I was going to be alright. How could a person who had spent nearly two decades in the same position not? I have been through every possible scenario and came out like a rose. Why wouldn't this be any different.

Chapter 10

A few more weeks had passed. I had pulled myself away completely from my daily conversations with Alec. I had not figured out if it was for him or me. The mental burden of uncertainty that was engulfing me appeared to be worse. The "intern" and the "hamster" shared very little information with me on any front. The calls with the "hamster" and the weekly meeting with the intern became more of a cat-and-mouse session. I would ask questions; they would deflect. I would offer suggestions, and they would repel. I would get off the call to feel worse than before. My daily routine was as disjointed as I started to turn more to my Vivant team for a sense of comfort. Most were going along with the changes, but I could tell the stress and uncertainty was building. A few had told me that Alec had reached out to discuss his retirement to try and assure them that everything would be OK. The theme that continued to come back to me from his conversations was, "I could have sold the company to someone else, and they would have gotten rid of all of you." This floored me. Is Alec trying to make us all believe he did the employees, me, and the company a favor? Selling to Dan Rand is why we all still have a job? Who is this man I trusted, putting my entire life and career into his hands? The weight was starting to get heavier on my mind, and I was losing more sleep to try to keep my head above water.

Waking on another Friday to a view of a much-needed weekend, I had to prepare for what would be known as the "All Team Meeting." This would be my first chance to see everyone in one place. I knew there was another wing of the Comptor empire. I checked the Zoom invite, and we had 197 employee invites. Most were names I did not recognize. I was the one who used to prepare these meetings; I would call them, agenda it out, and run the entire show. Today, I was just another spectator. I was looking at this meeting as an opportunity to be introduced as the highest-ranking remaining member of Vivant. I am sure this is why Dan has not really made any comments to or about me yet. He wanted to wait for this venue. Being a professional and a seasoned businessman, these are the optics that he wanted to present to his and my former team. I sat at my computer a few minutes before the start of the meeting and adjusted my screen so I looked even in the frame. Showered, clean shirt, brushed teeth. I was mentally preparing for an introductory speech. I took a few notes not to forget what I wanted to say. I was ready to give my speech to the "Academy." "Thank you all, you like me, you really like me," as Sally Field once said with her gold statuette. I was brimming with enough confidence to think that this afternoon's meeting would change my life and outlook. Big breath, saddle in, here we go.

The "intern" started the meeting. She made some initial introductions. She made sure she let everyone know that she was running this conference. Dan interjected; he wore a blue Nike T-shirt, sunglasses on his head, hair ruffled.

"Hello, everyone, and welcome. This is an incredibly exciting day for me and the company. My dream of purchasing Vivant began almost three years ago. I have been in partnership with Alec Teacham on other accounts, and we started discussions. With the help of Ali Howard, Laura Staley, and many others behind the scenes, we got this over the finish line. I appreciate Alec and his guidance throughout this journey. Him being the sole owner and only person to build up this great company is something I admire so much. I could not imagine doing all that work alone."

I felt blood rush out of my face. I looked at my reflection on the computer screen and tried everything I had not to break down or leave the room. I had never felt so sick, and my head was trying desperately not to spin. The following 10 minutes of the meeting were a blur. All I could hear was like an old Peanuts cartoon when the adults started speaking, "Wah...Wah...Wah, Wah, Wah." I brought myself back when Dan began calling on the staff shoutouts.

"I know a merger of this magnitude takes a village, and I wanted to point out someone who has been instrumental over the first six weeks since we took this over. Laura Staley, I appreciate you so much. Your hard work and incredible sense of humor always keep me grounded. Your leadership with the Vivant team has been exceptional."

AND....I thought.

"I want to thank you all for being a part of this first meeting of the Comptor-Vivant team. I look forward to seeing you all again, and please reach out to me if you ever want to have virtual coffee. I am a big fan of that. Bye for now."

That was it. Within seconds, all 196 people dropped off. I was just staring at the screen—the only one left. The last man virtually standing. I could not even access my shock when my phone began to blow up. "What was that??" from one employee. "Laura Staley? She has been talking shit about me for weeks now." from another. "You have a really bad poker face; I could see you wanted to reach through and strangle Dan," from a third. I answered as I always did, professionally, and took the high road. I have always been cognizant as a leader to be able to rise above the fray, no matter how much I may be affected personally. This time was the toughest of them all. For the first time, the word "betrayed" solidified in my head. Alec never let me know anything about this. My theories of why he was selling were completely off. I had initially thought Alec was just given an offer he could not refuse. Something that came up out of the blue, and he made an emotional decision. This was him instantly winning the lottery. I could have somewhat understood that. A three-year plan to get out? This I could not understand. I googled "betrayal" just to make sure I was on the right track. The action of betraying one's country, a group, or a person; treachery: the example they provided "the betrayal by the king by his daughter." All I saw was "the betrayal by Alec to me." I crumpled up my notes for the speech I was never able to give, then turned off my computer.

Chapter 11

I struggled through the following week. Employees came to me for answers I could not provide. My distrust of the "hamster" disconnects with the "intern." I was trying to figure out how I would confront Alec about all of this. He was trying to connect with me each day, and I ignored him. I was not ready to throw my grenade at him. I do not see this situation as being sustainable. The only question is, how long can I hold out? Since that meeting the previous week, I had lost all passion or motivation on any level for this job. This was a "job" now. In 20 years as Operations Director, I never referred to this as a job. This was my career, my future, my identity. As hard as I struggled at times, I always gave my best to it because I cared. Not just about the work itself. It was the vision. It was Alec. He was my hero, my mentor, and one of the best people I had ever known. I fear that he will spin this back at me when I confront him. I knew Alec better than he knew himself. When we had to make tough decisions about people in his life, personally or professionally, he knew how to frame that person in a way where Alec always looked good, and the other person looked bad. Maybe that is why I am fearful. I am on the other end of this now. I cannot be emotional; I must address him on his terms. That is the only way I can get through to him.

All of this reminds me why I never confronted my ex-wife about why she left me. She would have refused, spin it all on me. Did Alec just leave me the same way? Selfishly with no thought of the repercussions to someone else. A person so committed. Love and loyalty can hurt in so many ways when it goes bad. I am so anxious, but it needs to be done. I need to take a stand no matter what happens. To be respected, I need my own respect. I did not do that with my ex and need to do that here.

I have spoken to colleagues in my industry during the last seven weeks to know if my feelings are real and valid. My frustration, anger, and humiliation have boiled over to now. I feel there is no going back. I will be me. I will still do my job my way, the right way.

I Finished another week. Still stewing, continue to ignore Alec. The heat in my head keeps boiling. It is time to let the person know they were wrong just to assume I would be OK with this decision. As good as I am at torturing my own soul, the time has come to make the first contact. I will do it in email correspondence. I need to be strategic about each word. Alec can twist; I understand that about him.

Chapter 12

I spent the entire weekend contemplating what I would say to Alec. I spent two decades with this man. Now, as I prepare to get some answers for what has happened to the company, him, and me, I know Alec so well; his charm can be used for good, and I have seen it used not for evil but for "finesse." Finesse was always how Alec described, telling people what they needed to hear to push the agenda in our direction. He used it on clients and employees with a precision that left me in awe at times. As impressive as it is, I always feared that I would not want him to ever use it on me. I felt, in ways, that I knew Alec better than he knew himself. That was something that I took pride in, yet now it seems frightening. I sat at my computer, preparing to craft one of the most critical correspondences of my life.

Alec,

As you know, I have not spoken to you in a few weeks. I have not answered your calls or texts. I have been trying to figure out how to address many issues with you about what happened over the last two months. This has been one of the most challenging times of my career.

I am still trying to understand why this happened. I have attempted to settle into my new position, whatever that may be. I have gotten little guidance, and I feel my experience has not been valued since this merger happened.

I have spoken to many people over the last several weeks, and I think I have figured out how this went down. It is entirely different than my theories about why you decided to sell. I am troubled at why you left me in the dark about this for 3three years.

This was not the plan. Our plan. I understood if you wanted to step back, I was supposed to step in. We have discussed this at times over the years. The trust we had developed was something that meant the most to me about our relationship.

I understand that this is your company, and you can do with it what you will. You do know that I am the only person who believes in this as much as you do. I have prepared for years to carry on your legacy. This was my dream.

I feel lost as each day passes. You know more about my personal struggles than any other person. My Divorce destroyed me. The family members lost during the pandemic. I poured my life into work. This company, this vision. This is my passion. I believed in something bigger than myself.

You taught me to suppress my pain and channel my energy into the positive. I have done that for years now. That is all gone, and all I feel is despair.

I just need, no, I demand an explanation. I have never asked anything of you over the years. I trusted you to care for me, and you did so on so many occasions. This one time, as you ride off into the sunset, I insist that you tell me what happened—the truth. I have earned that right.

Thank You.

I stared at the email for almost 20 minutes, got up from my chair, paced the room, and sat back down again. If I smoked, I would have chained at least 6 in that time and watched the blinking cursor over and over again. Finally, I pressed send, off into hyperspace. As I slumped back in my chair, I realized I wasn't anxious about what I had written; it was more about the response.

After two days, I still had not heard from Alec. Things were beginning to devolve very quickly in all aspects of my life. I had begun to become unhappier with each day. I am in a place where I almost want to sabotage my work. Maybe I will get fired, and I can escape this. I keep thinking about the email I sent him and conclude that I may not get the answers I am looking for. I am so fearful he won't get it. He will spin as Alec has done before. This time, I will be the victim of the "finesse." I hate how this engulfs every minute of my days. I need to clear my mind in the worst way. I do not see a clear path out of this. I am still stunned that my feelings mean nothing to anyone in this company—especially the one man who once meant the most.

On the 4th day, I woke up to see an email from Alec in my box. I stood up to leave my home office. I was not ready to open it. I took a walk. When I returned, I made my way back to my desk and clicked on the response.

Hello

I am going to give you a few thoughts about the email you sent me a few days ago. I have been extremely busy and had to prioritize some other things.

Over the last twenty years, we have had an exceptional work relationship and friendship. I am sorry you are so frustrated with your new job position and are upset with me. I never intended for those things to happen.

You are correct; this was my company, and I had a right to what was best for me and my family. To be even more clear, Dan Rand is the new owner and has taken over the company. He knew you were my "right-hand man." It is up to him now how the company is run. I felt confident handing the company over to Dan because of the management of his company and our past partnerships over the last ten years.

I don't know where you learned about how this whole thing went down. You should have known I wanted to get out and spend more time with my family. I do not understand where you thought I was planning on handing the company over to you. I wanted to get out of daily operations and do other things with my life,

I did not tell you anything because I signed a non-disclosure agreement, and although I wanted to discuss this with you, I was instructed not to.

I hope this clarifies some things for you, and I am sorry you are having a rough time with all of this. Call me if you want to discuss further.

A.

I sat at my computer, stunned. Again, watching the cursor blink over and over. I had to look it over again to be sure. My anxiety was not a sham at all. This was real. He did it. I was nothing. I did all I could not to go into a panic attack. My emotions were going in directions I never fathomed. I felt pain, anger, despair, helplessness. I was nowhere near what to harness. I did not know what to expect with the response, but this was not it. Betrayed. I fell to the floor and wept. During this barely coherent session of sobbing, I could not help but get taken back into the soup of my past. My dad, my wife. "When you need me, I will be there," the old man told me. "I love you more than life itself; you are everything to me," she said on my wedding day, embraced on the dance floor. I let it happen again. Pathetic. I have the conviction of a child as a middle-aged man. I lay staring at the ceiling for what felt like hours. Catatonic. Almost in a trance. I could not feel my limbs, my head, or my heart. I dozed off well past the time I should have been in bed. I had a sore neck, back, and spirit when I woke—I had to rally. Life wasn't going to feel sorry for me. I did have an answer to my immediate problem. Loyalty. Now, I had to see what lay ahead. Survival. Without any support, I was aiming low.

Chapter 13

As I slept, I dreamed of my own funeral. A part of my heart had died the day before. I was running out of heart to die. So many had killed pieces of it. We were now at a point where an obituary may be in order.

Aeron Harmon's heart, 50, passed away on October 2nd, 2022, due to stabbings from people he trusted. Even though he had a susceptible heart, it was taken from this world. His loving nature and loyal heart left a beacon of light for all but was neglected by most.

This heart is survived by no one, and its once loving wife left him, his best friend let him down, and his mentor betrayed him. It was the vessel of a once proud man who tried to live his life with integrity. Unfortunately, no one will remember him or his heart. It will be dust kicked down the road. The remnant has blown around for eternity. Good riddance.

A small gravesite service for his heart will be held on October 5th, 2022, at the city cemetery, but it should not last long because no one will show up. Why would they?

At that moment in the dream, I saw the face of "The Tall Man" from the 1970 horror classic Phantasm shovel the first clump of dirt on my face, and I woke up in a drenching sweat. This was about to be another banner day.

I was called into a meeting this morning with the "hamster" and "intern" to discuss what the company's organizational chart was going to look like. Another Zoom call and no Dan Rand. After some brief pleasantries and a screen share, I looked at where I was on the pecking order. Line 4 of the chart. At the top was Rand. The second Line was the "intern." The "hamster" 2 other females and a male that I did not recognize. Line 4 and I was jumbled with 5 others, all females. Each had titles, except me.

"So, we need to figure out how you fit in," the "intern" said.

"Yeah, we have been trying to figure out for weeks now where we want to put you," replied the "hamster."

The "Intern" was even more stern, "I know you did a lot for Vivant, and Alec has told me you were his right-hand man, but I don't exactly know what that means. I guess if you handled operational things, what did that look like?"

"I did everything, Ali. Everything." I tried not to explode through the screen.

"Yeah, I know, but what did you do?" she questioned.

"Ali, we were a small business. We did not have departments. I was the departments; I was the infrastructure. I handled hiring, firing, payroll, and employment reviews. I was the motivational speaker and the sounding board. Every decision made in this company the 20 years I had a say in. Does that answer your question?" I could not have spoken more sternly.

"Uh huh, I get that…Let me ask another way. What are you good at?"

"Everything, Ali." A momentary pause came over the screens.

"Okay, I know you are a great communicator, and the employees respect the hell out of you." The "hamster" chimed in, feeling the tension.

Another pause. No one could look at each other. I stared at the cursor on my office computer as I squirmed and thought. The cursor was starting to give me more comfort than it deserved.

"Ali, I have always been told I am great at interviewing and finding the right staff to do the job we need done. Can I ask? Why have none of you had any idea what my role with this company is going to be?"

"That's why we are here now." That statement tore through me. These were who I will be answering to now, and neither have a clue. The Chief of Staff in her 20s, one step away from running this multi-million-dollar company, has no idea how to use someone with at least triple the experience as her. I just blurted something out.

"How about Staffing Director? I can focus on the hiring process. It is what I am good at, so why don't we go with that."

"Perfect. Nice job. I knew we could come up with something here. Laura, can you add to the chart and create a job description?"

"I can do the job description, Ali. It is my position." I uttered.

"No, we got it. I will send it to you, and you can add anything you think is relevant."

The "intern" quickly let us both know she had another meeting and dropped off. It was just me and the "hamster."

"Laura, why hasn't anyone thought about me at all here? We are 2 plus months in, and there has not been a discussion. And why hasn't Dan reached out to me at all yet?" I was visibly perplexed.

"Look, there is so much going on behind the scenes here that we are just kind of dealing with situations as they come along," she expressed, not very confidently.

"I know, Laura, I get it, but why the hell am I not on any of these internal phone calls, meetings, client decisions. I know what I am doing. I can help."

"Don't worry about it. Let me go so I can get these requests done, and we can talk tomorrow." She was ready to get off the screen, and she dropped.

I just shook my head. If anyone tells me to "Not Worry About It" again, I swear. I am starting to discover that another phrase for "Fuck You" is "Don't Worry."

Chapter 14

A few days later, my phone rang. It was Mary Fable. She is an incredibly talented person who was at the top of my list of most respected colleagues. She saved me many times while we were trying to stay afloat during the pandemic. I was fiercely loyal to her. She was running a virtual department for Vivant before the merger and is now trying to negotiate a new position with Comptor. It was not going well.

"Hey Aeron, I had to call you. They are making my life hell right now. Constant back and forth, multiple people. No one is on the same page about anything, and they just sent me these 12 pages of a non-compete." Her voice shook.

"Non-Compete? Seriously. We have never made our employees sign a non-compete before. Can you send it to me?"

She proceeded to email the document...I mean documents. I read through this and was shocked. I've never read through anything like this before. The company was looking to force her to practically give up her career for 2 years if she left or was let go. All the materials she created were no longer hers. Scrub her business and social media accounts clean and be re-written by the company. I called her back.

"This is nuts, Mary. I have never seen a document like this in my career, ever!"

"I don't know what to do. Can you help me?" she asked.

"Yes, no problem."

I went through the documents with her and walked through options for requesting items to be removed and/or reworded. There was quite a bit to be reworked. As I was looking over the documents, I was beginning to think: Is this something we are all going to have to sign at some point? I refocused on Mary and what she needed to do to protect herself. After about an hour, we were done, and she thanked me.

"I appreciate this. Look, can we talk later or tomorrow? There are some things I have noticed and just want to run by you." There was concern in her voice, and I knew this next conversation might be a key to something.

"Sure, call me anytime. I will find time for you." We said our goodbyes, and I sat back again at my desk. Falling physically deeper into my seat. I could feel my anxiety kicking in. I hate the unknown, I despise change, and every minute, my life is spiraling into this bewilderment. How is it that everything was good barely 8 weeks ago but is now in this place? Not having any sense of what is happening. Having to deal with the ineptitude of this group. Middle age does not deserve this.

Chapter 15

"Follow me. Shhhh. Just follow me." I walk along this dark, narrow hallway. A voice keeps speaking to me to follow her. She sounds so familiar. I keep walking. *"I love you and will take care of you. Just follow me."* I keep moving. The light is dim. I pass by several doors. I grab the knobs of a few. They are locked. I keep walking. A thick mist starts to take over, and I see very little in front of me. *"I will take care of you. Just follow me."* The voice does not stop. I am drawn to it. Soothing. Caring. Real. I want to touch the voice. Feel it. Embrace it. *"I will never hurt you. You are my one and only. You are everything. Come to me, my love."* I started to move quickly through the hallway. I cannot see through the Mist. I have no direction, and I move faster, from walking to jogging to sprinting. *"Come to me, my love. I need you so much."* I begin to cry as I move faster and faster down the hallway. *"I will protect you from all. You are the one, the only one."* The Mist and the tears take over, and I feel like I am going nowhere down this hallway. When will it end? I need to see. To feel. To touch this voice. I know this voice. I yell out, *"I am coming, I am coming. I need you too."* My breathing becomes labored. *"You are so close, my love; do not give up. I will protect you."* I come to the end. The Mist disappears. A door is in front of me. I grabbed the knob. It turned. I let it go as the door opens. *"Come to me, my love. I am waiting."* I take a step. There

is no floor, and I fall. I reach my hands to grab something. One hand and I somehow hold onto what feels like a ledge. I reach up with my other hand and grip both as tight as I can. The darkness of the room scares me. I feel a hand grabbing for me. I let the hand pull me up. As I am pulled out of the hole, I see a light and then a face. Then two. "You sorry bastard, You pathetic little worm." It is the "intern" snakes in her hair. "Let's stew him up." The "hamster" chimes in while I see my ex-wife towering over both, a greasy, Cheshire smile on her face...

I fell out of bed, hitting my head on the nightstand. As I pop up, the clock reads 3:03 am. I am sweaty and peed my pants. My god, what is happening to me?

I spent the next 3 hours just lying on the floor, trying to get back to sleep. No avail. At 6:15 am, I just decided that this was over. I made my way out of bed. I am feeling the first signs of insanity trying to push its way in. Moving my way into the living room, I sit on the couch, then lay my head in my hands to beg for help. "Why, Why, is this happening?" I get no answer, of course. I lay back for a minute. Then, decided to make a pot of coffee. Large pot. I am going to need it today.

Mary called me around 11:30 am. I was thinking about this all morning after the dream I had overnight; it was certainly a little edgy.

"Hi Mary, how are you this morning?"

"Fine, you sound rough. Are you doing okay?" she responded concerned.

"Yeah, just dreams and stuff. I am fine. What's on your mind today?"

"Well, I have been wanting to talk to you for a while. Laura is driving me nuts. I can't do my job. This is non-compete aside. I am being micromanaged with everything I do. Alec, just let me do my job. This is insane right now."

"I know, things are different now. Can I ask if you have spoken to Alec lately? He and I are not talking right now."

"Not really? Literally, the day after the merger went down, he just disappeared. We were working on all these new contacts and initiatives, and it was just not his problem anymore. He has called me a few times, but not to talk about anything work-related."

"Are you kidding me, Mary? I just don't understand what the hell is going on. It is like Alec isn't the same person we all worked for anymore."

"I know. Can I tell you something, too? This is Dan Rand. What a holy roller he is. Every meeting I am on with him, he has to pray, and Ali and Laura go along with it. Totally inappropriate."

"Hmm, I knew he was born again but didn't know how far he took it. He does this before you start a meeting?" My mind was starting to churn.

"Yeah, but only when both Ali and Laura are our Zooms. If I do a meeting with just him and one of them, he doesn't do it. Very odd."

"I'll say. Is Alec on any of these meetings with you, and does he do it with him, as well?"

"No, but he does this sign of the cross thing and kisses his fingers and touches his heart. But only when Alec is on a call. He has even tried to engage with me about my family's religious standing."

"Really?? What is up with that? More than inappropriate, this is just flat-out weird."

Mary was starting to really open up to me now. "Have you seen the organizational chart for the company? I went into the Comptor employee directory on the website. Almost every employee is a woman and young, too. I hate to say it, but he seems to be more comfortable around younger women. He seems intimidated by me or at least uncomfortable. I know I am 53, but the last thing anyone would say about me is that I am intimidating." Mary gave a half-sarcastic laugh.

"I am stunned by this, Mary. Alec has given me no answers and no direction. I don't feel like I even know him anymore. I am angry and frustrated and feel like I have no idea where I stand now."

"You should check out the employee directory, and it is pretty interesting. Can you please talk to Laura and tell her to get off my back? I just want to do my job and be left alone. I took care of the non-compete stuff. I signed it with a couple of changes." Mary had a bit of resignation in her voice.

"I wish you would have had someone else look at it, Mary. I have real problems with the document and hope this isn't sprung on all of us."

"I know. I just didn't want to stress out about it. So much is going on. Hey, I need to go now, but let's catch up again in the next week." Mary hung up the phone.

I immediately went to the employee portal on the Comptor site. Started counting. Got up to 197 employees. Only 7 men and that included Dan. From the faces, none of the females looked older than 30. No diversity. Not one person of color, either. How can you run a company of this size with so much inexperience? None of the employees on our side were on the site yet. Our demographics were close to 50/50 male and female, which is what you would expect. I would hire anyone who I felt could do the job. Comptor seems to have a different dynamic for employee recruitment. I did not know what to make of this. Thoughts were creeping in that I did not fit the mold of what this company was looking for. Maybe this is why things have been so difficult. How could Alec not notice any of this and feel it was strange, at the very least?

Chapter 16

I spent the next few weeks trying to settle into what was approaching or what would come next. I am coming to terms with the fact that my relationship with Alec is over, and I am okay with it. I feel that I can never trust him again. With the ability to cut people out of my life, he is done and gone. He has never dealt with someone like me who can eliminate people like they never existed. I have emotionally been able to remove people from my life with a simple philosophy. Eliminate the person and suppress the feeling. I have gotten really fucking good at it. So many people have gone into that black hole and never returned. No regrets. Alec is no different than anyone else. I did this to my family, best friend, ex-wife, all of them. You fuck me, and you are gone, period. No reprieve, no forgiveness. I have no patience for bullshit or spin. This still does not answer the questions I have about what has happened with our highly successful company. How could it be taken over by people who clearly have no idea what they are doing?

I finally changed my work status to Staffing Director...so what? Updated the social media accounts. I guess I just needed to do it to move on from what I once was. As expected, Alec flubbed and "congratulated" me on what is technically a demotion. The relationship is over. He is as much of a clueless emotional person as my ex-wife. I think I am okay with something and have absolutely no empathy for what I am really going through. I have finally settled into what I am and what I mean to this company. From what I am seeing all around me, the end will come, and I know it, but I can't worry anymore. I just need to accept where and what it will be. I have to say my emotions are starting to twist me in the wind. I broke down after stumbling onto an old Jessie J song that always spoke to me and my ex. Listening to "Domino" took me back to our car karaoke days on a Friday night, coming home from a baseball game or concert. It is still overwhelming. I lost it. Crying seems easier and easier as the losses mount.

The self-evaluation of my own job working with two women who have no clue what they are doing. Making me use worthless recruitment platforms that provide me with little to no candidates who can do the jobs we need to get done. What I have seen in recent weeks is the most troubling. Our account contracts are being cut and not negotiated properly. Dan and his team have done nothing to establish or nurture any relationships with the clients we have had for as long as I have worked with Vivant. They have decided not to let the only face remaining from the old regime participate in any of the negotiating or client relation processes. This, in turn, has caused upheaval internally with the current employees and has made my responsibility of staffing nearly impossible. Is this a setup to fire me? Or has the ineptitude reached a tipping point? I made an appointment with the Comptor HR manager to express my concerns but then thought better of it and decided to just go in the direction of mental health. My emotional struggles are at a level I have never experienced. I go back to the first "All Team Meeting" in September. Learning the truth about the merger. I felt a pop like an athlete who blows out an ACL. They knew it when it happened. "Heard a pop." That "pop" went off in my brain, and I have not been the same. The nightmares, sleeplessness, weight loss. I was withering away in real-time. That is what I addressed with this HR manager. The result and not the cause. She proceeded to give an HR spiel, take a report, and send me a link to a chaplain service provided by the company. I have a feeling she wanted me to "Pray it away." No mental health services, just a church ritual? Again, I was on my own.

Chapter 17

The next few days were the same futile process. Ramp up to work, have no direction on what is next, and deal with the "hamster" phone call at the end of the day. I had just got done with her and was settling into the end of the day with another very strong drink when my phone went off. "Hey, it is Jeff. Can we talk?" This was Jeff Peoples, one of the longest-tenured managers working for us. I brought him over nearly 12 years earlier. He was young, green, with a lot of family baggage. He is a great kid, well, not really a kid anymore. He is 30. I had watched him mature before my eyes and had overseen his growth as an employee and as a man. I had a soft spot for him as much as anyone who had ever worked for us. I texted back, "Sure, call me whenever you are ready." The phone rang almost immediately.

"Hey Aeron, what is going on?"

"Alec called me today. I haven't talked to him since this damn merger went down. He seems to be fishing for something." Jeff had a combination of concern and disdain in his voice.

"I think Alec is trying to figure some things out. I am not talking to him anymore. He fucked us all over, Jeff"

"You are not kidding; he was trying to sell me on how lucky we all are that he let Dan buy his company and how much it saved our jobs. I don't trust that bastard."

"I know. Alec seems to be justifying all of this to everyone." I sounded resigned, sadly.

"Check this out: they asked me to be on a bunch of these social media committees, and one of them is this prayer group. Everyone in this group is all under 30, and most are the women who work on the Comptor side."

"Really, I have not heard about this group."

"Yeah, and Tom wants to join it just to fuck with these people."

Tom Timlin was a former intern who worked his way to run one of the most successful contracts in the company. He was a bit of a knucklehead when he came on board, but I have grown so fond of him that I looked at him as my "pseudo son." He had matured greatly over the 10 years he worked for us in every possible capacity. With his maturity, he didn't lose his ability to get under someone's skin and take the other side of an argument for the hell of it. He is also an atheist, so the religious side of Dan Rand was something that really rubbed him. I could see him getting into a prayer group just to cause trouble.

"I know Tom, and I could see that, big time. I don't understand all this religious stuff. Dan is a little whacked out with all of this."

"I hate these meetings where he has to start with a prayer. It is like he has no respect for anyone's feelings and just needs to do this. I hate it." Jeff sounded very irked by all of it.

"Is this the only reason why you called?" I asked.

"No, it is about Laura Staley. Mary sent me text screenshots of her trashing me about some stupid presentation that I didn't do exactly how she wanted me to. What the hell is her problem, and can you get her off my back? This is utter bullshit."

"I will see what I can do, Jeff. I am getting a lot of complaints lately." My loss of internal company power made me less confident about that statement than I would otherwise have been.

"Thanks. What should I do about Alec? I don't want to talk to him anymore."

"Just ignore him, Jeff. That is what I am doing." I took a big breath and ended the conversation.

I needed to get more information about this "prayer group." Hearing this from two of my most accomplished employees and being offered it myself from H.R. was incredibly strange. I decided to reach out to Tom. I kept it in a text stream.

"Hey Tom, I just talked to Jeff. He told me you are looking to go "knucklehead" on this Comptor prayer group ☺ "

"Ha Ha, hell yes. I love f-ing with these douches. LMFAO"

"Have you been a part of a meeting yet?"

"Yeah, last week, so weird, mostly chicks, nobody really talked, it was like some kinda sermon. The leader of the group looks like she is 21. Ali Howard was in it, too. She was wearing this weird parka-type thing. Looked like something a Nun on leave would wear. LMAO ☺"

"Did you do or say anything?"

"No, it was too odd for me. I just dropped off after about 20 minutes. Way too intense."

"Gotcha, are you going back?"

"Hell No!! Done with that. Hey, gotta go. Come by and see me later this week if you are not busy."

"Sure, later."

Don't know what to make of all this. We were heading into Thanksgiving week, and I just got called into an emergency meeting with the "intern" and the "hamster." Couldn't stop thinking about the intern dressing like a Nun.

Chapter 18

A Monday morning meeting. Hopped onto a Zoom, and they were both in the normal place. The "intern" in her living room is wearing something that someone in her position should not be wearing, somewhat of a nightgown-looking shirt and a plate of food in full view. The "hamster" in her basement and ¼ of her face cut out of the frame. She never lines herself up correctly on any of these calls.

"So, to get started, we have been negotiating this Hospital contract that you have been managing. They want to pull the plug on Marcus." The "intern" finished before taking a bite of her burrito.

Marcus is one of the company's most decorated employees. A former military academy man, he served in the first and second Iraq wars and was a born leader like few I had ever worked with. He was an older, very well-built African American who was easy to talk to and like. He was our account lead before the pandemic, and when that account ended, we were contracted to provide staffing during the height of hospital admissions. Marcus was helping in several departments and was well respected by every supervisor at the hospital. He had maintained his position for nearly two years, and we were trying to help transition him out and into something more associated with his skill set.

"Why do you they want to pull the plug on Marcus, Ali?" I said sternly.

"We tried, and they just don't have the funds to keep him."

"Why wasn't I on any of these negotiating calls? I have worked on this account going back almost 8 years."

"That's not your job, that's mine."

"Yeah, OK, now what, Ali? What time frame are we looking at? It is Thanksgiving week; can we at least get him to the end of the year?"

"We discussed that, and they want to do this now." She could not be more heartless in her statements.

"So, you want to lay him off now?"

"We can let him know Tuesday."

"During a holiday week, really??"

"Let's say we pay him through the end of the week."

"How generous of you." I laid on the sarcasm as thick as I could muster.

"We will call him today. Laura, don't we have another position we can offer him?"

I jumped in.

"Hold on, Laura. Yeah, Ali, we have a position, but it is almost a 40% pay cut, and he will have an hour's commute back and forth. It is an insult."

Laura chimed in, "At least he will still have a job."

"You two are unbelievable. This is a man's life you are messing with here. Do you have any idea what Marcus did for us and how much money he has generated for this company? He took every vaccine and worked in about as dangerous of conditions as you could imagine at the height of the pandemic. He made such an impact; they created a position for him when they pulled the plug on the pandemic era position." I pleaded with them.

"That's nice. There is nothing we can do. We will call him today."

"No, Ali, I will call him. For chrissakes, I owe him that. I am staffing. I will deal with this."

"Are we done here?" Ali abruptly stated. "I have another meeting I need to get on."

She dropped off, and it was just me and the "hamster."

"Laura, are you OK with all of this? What the hell happened in the damn contract negotiations."

"Nothing unusual. I guess it's just economics."

"No, Laura, this is not just economics. Alec and I never handled things like this. These are people's lives, not a fucking bunch of numbers. I got to go. I will call Marcus in the morning and direct him to H.R. after."

"OK, talk tomorrow." Her lighthearted, clueless response was more than expected.

I was now in a position to make one of the more difficult calls in my career. I closed my day on my couch with a double shot of tequila and an Imperial IPA. I know those would not be the only drinks consumed tonight.

Chapter 19

Another sleepless night. The anxiety was becoming more than I could bear. The anger was bubbling. The helplessness had taken over. I felt I was still a little drunk from the night before. I stumbled out of bed at 5:45 am. I plunked down on the couch and watched the news for the next hour and a half with little interest. The stories of Holiday preparations, city shootings, and the upcoming Black Friday storm kept my mind off the task at hand. The local news moved into Good Morning America. More of the same. I had enough and jumped in the shower. Another half hour of everything washed over me.

I began to cry. For what specific reason I did not know. The headache, buzz, and exhaustion had taken over. I slowly sank into the tub, holding my knees to my chest and sobbing until I could not bear it anymore. The water began to turn cold, and I bailed on my despondency. I had to make the call and get it done with. I texted Marcus. He responded, and we set up a 10:00 am call. Another 2 hours wait. I poured my second cup of coffee and decided to go for a walk. Sitting in my empty home office wasn't doing me any good. I made it back in at 9:57, and subsequently, the phone rang. Marcus is always a little early when we set up calls, which is what you would expect from a military man. I pick up.

"Morning Marcus." Trying to be cheerful

"Good morning. What is up? Haven't spoken in a while."

"Yeah, I know, Marcus, apologize for that. Unfortunately, this is not a good news conversation."

"Oh, is this about the hospital?"

"Yes, I spoke with Ali yesterday, and they are closing the account and your position."

"Wow, that is a surprise and quick, too. I have been working on so much for the Trauma department. We were getting ready to ramp up this great new program for patients with PTSD."

"Really?" I was very surprised to hear this. "Ali and Laura never mentioned anything to me about this yesterday."

"They should have known about it. Isn't Helen Mercurial on the contract committee? She heads up Trauma."

"Yes, Marcus, I know that. This sounds like a real quality program that they should have wanted to get started."

"What does this mean? When am I being moved?"

"Tomorrow is the last day. They gave no grace or transition period on this thing."

"So, am I being transferred?"

"All I have, Marcus, is this support position in the city. About 40% less than you make now."

"So, the cord is being cut tomorrow, and I don't have a full-time job anymore?" His voice reflected anger in a way I had not heard the entire time I had known him.

I swallowed hard and tried to fight the oncoming nausea that was coming over me. "Yes, that about covers it." I was sick.

There was a pause for close to 30 seconds before he responded. "All right, I understand. What is going on with this company? What do I do now? Alec had been talking to me about another business opportunity working with the V.A., and now he doesn't return my calls."

"How long ago was that?" I asked.

"3 months."

"My god, really? I thought Alec was only doing this to me." I sighed hard enough for Marcus to pick up on it.

"You sound pretty frustrated."

"I don't know what to think anymore, Marcus. What has happened to this company and all of us is insane."

"So, what do I do now?"

"H.R. is going to reach out to you after I let them know you are not going to take the other position. You will be laid off and can collect unemployment."

"I still have a week's vacation; can I at least get that?"

"That should not be a problem. I will let them know. You earned the time, so it is a no-brainer."

"OK, Thanks. I appreciate you calling me." He spoke as sincerely as he could in the moment.

"Marcus, I had to be the one to call you. I have so much respect for everything you have done for me and the company. We all went through so much during the pandemic, and to stay afloat took a lot from all of us. I will never forget the work you put in."

We stayed on the phone silently for about another 30 seconds before saying goodbye. He made the call as endurable for me as he could. Marcus was that kind of person. I thought I would be relieved that the call was over. Instead, I was even more down, and the nausea took me to the bathroom, and I threw my guts up.

Chapter 20

I sent a message to HR to contact Marcus as I rallied to get on with the workday. My headache and nausea had subsided. I was preparing for a meeting with the staff to discuss prep for the yearly marketing plans we provide to all the clients. This is a roadmap for the year. More or less, what we will be doing to justify our contracts... Bottom line – What we are getting paid for. This also gives our leaders a chance to take control of their surroundings. It is part of my philosophy of leadership. Empower and support. Alec and I had nurtured that concept over many years. This allowed us to keep quality people longer than most companies in our industry. I began to reminisce for a moment. My phone went off. A text from Marcus.

"They are not going to pay me!"

"What do you mean, **not pay you?**" I returned.

"My vacation time I earned. They said it is in the employee handbook. If you leave or get laid off, you forego vacation time earned."

I knew that was not in our employee handbook, but I had not yet seen the "Comptor handbook." None of us have. It wasn't to be presented until after Thanksgiving.

"Marcus, I am going to talk to someone about this. You should get what you earned."

"Yeah, I know, the HR manager talked down to me like I was some kind of animal."

"OK, let me see if I can figure this out."

"Thanks."

I had no confidence I could figure anything out anymore. I connected with the HR manager and was referred to the handbook that I had not yet received. She explained the concept of company policy and gave me the "there is nothing I can do" spiel. I reached back out to the "intern" and the "hamster." They both gave me the same response. A statement from the "intern" during this conversation finally set me off, "He could have taken the other position, that is his issue, not ours." I was done. I threw my phone across the room. Thankfully did not break it but dented the shit out of the cell cover. It left a nice little dimple on my office wall. At that time as I picked up my dented phone off the carpet in my office I had received a text from Alec.

"Happy Thanksgiving week, bud!"

I stared at it as I paced the floor for almost five minutes before responding.

"Fuck you, Alec! you betrayed me, you bastard!"

Another five minutes went by.

"We need to talk tomorrow."

I responded immediately.

"Yes, we fucking do! It is time for a reckoning."

We decided to meet in the parking lot of our old office headquarters. The day before Thanksgiving, I never thought I would meet Alec under circumstances like this.

I woke, dressed, caffeinated up, and headed to my car. I made the 25-minute commute to the parking lot of the office we built this company on. The year prior I did this drive, but under much different circumstances. We met in our office ready to discuss football, share a beer or two, and feel grateful for the good fortune we have as friends and as a company. I now have nothing. My career and future are on life support. I am on the verge of despising the man who gave me my career. The hatred was starting to engulf me with each mile I drove. I pulled into the parking lot and was not surprised where Alec was stationed. The second spot, before the front door of the building. He had taken that place just about every chance he could get. It was never open when his car was in that lot. I parked in my favorite spot four down from him. We were the only cars on this cold morning. Most were either working from home or just calling it for the Holiday weekend. I sat in my seat, looked out onto the huge grassy property like I had hundreds of times before, took a breath, and prepared for the reckoning I had promised the day before. I got out of my car and made my way to his. Felt like gunslingers in the old west. We didn't have guns, just words, but they were to be just as deadly.

I stood before him and made my initial statement. "What the hell have you done to all of us, Alec? I had to let Marcus go yesterday. Do you have any fucking idea what is going on with this company?"

"I just want to let you know that when you use the words betrayal and reckoning, it really worries me and my family." A surprising response to my question.

"Did you hear what I just said? What the fuck are you worried about?"

"You just seem unstable right now, that's all."

"Alec, I am absolutely infuriated! I think I have a right after all of this. Every employee has come to me either mad or just goddamn confused with what these idiots at Comptor are doing! Do you understand that!?"

"I think you are just being overly emotional. I know how you can be. Dan and his team know what they are doing."

"For chrissakes! Shut up, Alec! Snap out of this! They don't know what they are doing. The morale of this company is crumbling around me. Plus, you realize that you did nothing to protect me or give me any leverage to push back on any decision-making internally with this group."

"I believe in Dan, he is the owner now and you need to just trust what he is doing. If we lose people, that happens in this type of situation."

"FUCK YOU, Alec! I cannot believe you are the same person I put all my trust in!" I was having an out-of-body experience with every word coming out of his mouth.

"See, this is what worries me. I know how emotional you are, my wife and girls are concerned you might do something you will regret."

I realized at that instance that I had just wasted my time. "Alec...you really don't care about any of us, do you? You didn't do anything to protect me or our people. Just why...Why!!"

"I did what I had to do to take care of my family. That's all that matters. If you can't fit into this "new normal", so to speak, I don't have time to worry about that."

I was speechless. He was mentally checked out. I just had to get the hell out of there. "Thanks, Alec, I appreciate knowing how you really feel. Happy Thanksgiving and kiss my ass." I walked away. Got in my car and squealed out. Hyperventilating for the first five minutes and trying to stay focused on the road, I was now in survival mode. What was I going to do? The only thing coming out of a Holiday weekend. I had to have a meeting with Dan Rand.

Chapter 21

I spent the Thanksgiving Holiday in one of the worst funks of my life. Spent the entire weekend alone. Thinking. Over thinking. Preparing. I started working on the letter to Dan on Friday morning. Black Friday! Fitting... I did not know how to start the letter, had to muster every ounce of my professional writing skill to try and encapsulate where I have been over the last four months. As I was writing, it dawned on me again that I have not had any one-on-one conversation with this man since the merger happened. I fought my growing anger to stay focused. I needed to make this as positive an experience as I could. So many were still depending on me to try and get things done. I wanted to be able to protect the employees who were struggling and that I cared for so much. This was a balancing act of my self-interest and for the people who would be left to burn, if I at least did not have some influence. I was looking at this letter and meeting as a reset. After several drafts, I finally had a worthy representation of my thoughts. Probably my full state of mind at the time. I slept on it Saturday night. Left it alone all Sunday. I took one last look before sending it out to Dan and the "intern."

Good morning,

I was hoping I could get a meeting to discuss my status with the company and several concerns I have.

After spending nearly four months working since the merger happened, I am struggling with what my role is with the company. I would have hoped for a conversation much earlier, yet I do understand there has been so much going on, that I put my concerns on the back burner.

The demotion to the "Staffing Director" is something I am struggling with. My expertise with the ins and outs of Vivants's operations is something that no one in your company has utilized or even discussed with me. This is highly disappointing since I know I could assist even more effectively with the transition.

I have spoken to many of our employees, and they have concerns about the status they have. The Non-compete Agreement and Standard Employment Agreement I have reviewed are making me a little uneasy since we can be released on an "At Will" basis and have to shut down our personal career opportunities for a minimum of 1 year.

The anxiety that I am dealing with has resulted in physical and emotional challenges that include weight loss, insomnia, and nightmares. I have been thinking about finding assistance to address some mental health issues I am currently going through. The transition from my former position as the number 2 person in Vivant to where I am now has brought me to a near-depressive state. My role for Vivant has defined me as a person and professional for nearly two decades and that is gone now. This is very difficult for me to share, but I think you should have a full flavor of what I am experiencing. I have felt a great deal of humiliation on many levels as I struggle to figure where I can be best utilized as part of the Comptor team.

All I am asking for is some clarity and hope to be considered with the value and respect that I believe I have earned while spending over a 1/3 of my life with this company.

I hope to talk to you soon. In the meantime, I will continue to deliver 100% to my position and assist in any way as this transition continues.

Aeron Harmon

I sit and look it over one more time before pressing "Send." I release it. My head drops to my chest. I looked back at the screen. I see the time in the right-hand corner of the computer. "10:38 pm." I needed to go to bed. I could only imagine what would be in my inbox in the morning.

I wake up several times during the night. Expected. I forced myself not to check the emails to see if there was a response. I was going crazy thinking about this. I am starting to come to terms with the fact that I need to get some help and be sincere about it. I have all the manifestations of anxiety, and low-grade depression that are starting to spiral out of control. I was not kidding in my letter or looking for sympathy. I was beginning to feel like I was in trouble. I must keep it together. So much to facet to keep the walls from closing in. I glance at the clock, "5:13 am." I drift back off.

"Hey, loser. Wake up." I open my eyes to see the "intern" floating above me. The "hamster" silhouetted behind her. My roof is gone, and I can see a clear night sky filled with stars. "You are such a pathetic piece of shit! You know we own you, just submit. It will make your life better." I tried to move, but I am stuck in the bed. I look up at the "hamster" and she keeps running in circles around the "intern." "You know I can break you. It is easy, just ask your wife." The "intern" lifts her shirt up to peel away the flesh from her abdomen and my ex-wife, Tara's face appears. The

intern drifts down and Tara comes nose to nose with me. "I never loved you."

I jerk and wake up. 6:02 am. I peed my pants again. I am a loser.

I rise and go directly into my office to check emails and nothing. I walk downstairs grab a 5-hour energy down in a gulp, and start the normal Monday routine. Local news, Good Morning America, check the FitBit sleep stats and heart rate, shower, shave, then head back into the office. The response arrived. First from Dan.

Thanks for your honesty. Hope you had a nice Holiday and let's definitely talk. Ali will set it up.

The "intern" responds about 30 minutes later.

Yes, Thanks, let's set up a meeting for 11:00 am tomorrow. I will send the invite.

Two lines! I spilled my guts and I got a two-line response. I guess I should not be surprised.

I woke early Tuesday, filled with the uncertainty of what to expect. I was glad we were doing this before lunch. After, I may have vomited again. Filled the first few hours of the workday with calls, and emails; the typical aspects of the job I think I was getting paid for. I pulled my iPad off my side desk. This is what I use to take Zoom calls, makes life easier, and leaves the laptop to deal with daily business. I pulled up my email on my computer, and logged into the Zoom call around 10:58. I like to be a little early. Both Dan and the "intern" arrived at precisely the same time. Just like a good, choreographed pair figure-skating side-to-side jump. The "intern," of course, had to speak first.

"Hey Aeron, how are you feeling?"

"Fine, thank you." I would rather Dan had spoken; he still had not had any conversation with me in nearly four months since the merger.

"Dan and I had read your email, and just wanted you to elaborate more about your feelings."

"OK, I think I made everything pretty clear, what more do you need?"

"I know this merger has been difficult for you, you have made that quite evident to a lot of people."

"You mean Laura?"

"Yeah, and others, too."

"I have always been an open book, Ali, anyone who knows me, knows that. I am not happy with some things going on here, but I put most of the onus of that on Alec."

Dan chimed in for the first time, "Alec is a good man, he knew what he was doing when we put all this together."

Dan's whole demeanor was irking me to no end. Blue T-shirt with a caricature sun and the slogan "Florida's calling." Black Oakley Sunglasses on his head, which needed a haircut desperately. His face wasn't centered on the screen, like the "hamster" on these calls. My shoulders were tensing with the stress of just the presentation. I tried to center my thoughts.

"Dan, I have no idea where I stand here. I spent nearly 20 years practically running this entire show, and in an instant, it was gone. I just want to know where I fit in."

"I know, I should have connected with you earlier, that is my fault."

The "intern" took over the call for the next 20 minutes and began a rambling diatribe about what the vision of the company was. The corporate buzzwords. She spoke of how the company needs to be more agile, technology-based, visual, and sustainable, that they need to move the needle, and that there was still a lot to unpack through the transition. Not once did she speak of people, human contact, or relationships. I fumbled with my hands, looked at the clock, and just wanted this to end.

Dan closed with his last response, "And with the will of God, of course."

"Yes, we believe that all things are created and inherited by God." Ali followed.

"Thank you, so what do you want me to do now?"

"Just your job. The employees respect you and what you say. Just reassure them that we are going in the right direction here."

"Can we talk about my finances for a sec? Did Alec say anything to you about this?"

"We found out about all that in the 11th hour, that was not a part of the negotiations. I am sorry, there is really nothing we can do. Your salary is still in place."

"Hold on a minute. Alec never mentioned any of the 'creative financing' he had done with me. This was helping to give him tax breaks, that is why I agreed to all of it. My retirement, vehicle, and insurance stipends, he didn't say anything about that? It is a significant amount of money."

"Nope, our accountant found some things and when we asked Alec, he just told us not to worry about it, you would understand."

"Ummm, OK, I guess I don't really understand!" I was boiling.

"Aeron, Dan has to get off and I have another meeting to jump on, are we good here?"

"Sure?" I stated.

"OK, Thanks for the time today." The "intern" dropped off first.

"Let's have virtual coffee soon, maybe after the Holidays?" Dan finished and then dropped off.

Holy shit, what a waste of time. Alec really did nothing for me. How much more do I need here? If I thought I was on my own before, I truly believed it now.

Chapter 22

This was the first time I had begun to think that my days were numbered. I have gotten no support from anyone, the feeling of being on an island alone is not a great way to get through the days. Having no power, say, or ability to help on any level is something I am not used to. Being helpless to solve any problems, have influence, leadership. Certainly not used to any of that. I have gone from being the "go-to" guy to being "nobody." This company does not want me. I am starting to see what they are trying to do. They want me out. They do not want to do it; they want me to. Make my life so miserable that I will decide to leave on my own. The misery is working, but I will not quit. This company has my handprints all over it. I will not relinquish it willingly. Fire me, I am not doing it for you. I am still the only conduit to protect my people, even if it is just providing whatever information I can gather. I must stay steadfast in hanging in, no matter how bad it gets. Make them do it. I don't think they will. I still have so much influence and information. Loyalty is something that Alec deserted, but not me. I owe it to myself and my team to gut this out no matter the consequences.

Although, I do think I need some professional help. I have not had to lean on therapy in over a decade. Tara insisted that I get help after my mother died. The abuse and neglect I had taken from my father as a child were starting to have negative effects on our marriage. Tara was the first person to help me address this. The decisions she made helped to put me in a better place for myself and our life together. I never believed I would have to probe this again. Her betrayal of me, Alec, and now with Comptor, has put me back in a place where I felt lost, and worthless. Funny how people can control like a puppet master, pull the mental strings of control. The rational and irrational mind has always been my struggle. I am rational, everyone around me puppets the irrational in my head. It is sad, the tender balance that has put me in a position where I am alone, physically and mentally. I miss Tara so much.

I woke up the next morning with several texts on my phone. Mary Fogle, Marcus, the "hamster," Tom Tinlin. He was the last one to come in. He would be the one I answered first. "You coming in today, I really need to talk." I simply responded, "Yes, around 10." I knew to come in at that time because he would be alone in his office. His assistant did not arrive until 11 am. It would have given me time to find out what was on his mind. Tom was someone who never took much seriously and had never told me he 'needed' to talk. So, I was more than curious to get into this. I arrived at his office. After a few chit-chat catch-ups, we got into it.

"What's on your mind, Tom?" In just about every conversation with an employee, I use that phrase. Seems like a great icebreaker, probably my calling card.

"Alec came by yesterday."

"Why?" I questioned.

"Good question. He said that he just missed coming to the client sites."

"That is odd, I thought he should be on a damn golf course somewhere."

"I asked him something like that, and he just said he missed this."

"So, is that what you wanted to tell me?"

"No, he just started rambling about you and spinning about all the changes."

"Me, what did he say about me?"

"He didn't understand why you are so mad, and that he did so much for you and if it wasn't for him, you never would be in the place you are now. It was like he was defending himself about something."

"You know why I am mad, Tom, right?"

"Absolutely! He is a fucking con artist and lied to all of us. I caught him in lies going back years, especially about what he was paying me. The client shared the contract with me, and I saw how much I was being lowballed. When I called him out on it, he was more upset about me seeing the information than the fact he was screwing me over."

"I think he had us all snowed, Tom. I bought his bullshit for years. He was using 'creative financing' with my salary, which helped him, more than me."

"To be honest, I never trusted him. He was a good talker, but I saw through most of it."

"Wish I did, Tom. I loved the man. You see what happened with that?"

"My condolences." He laughed a bit with that sharp comment.

"Fuck You, Tom," I laughed back at him.

"Seriously, what are you going to do?"

"I don't know, I think they want me to quit, but I ain't doing that. They gotta fire me. I feel like I am a dead man walking anyway."

"I figure that with you. Last thing, I want to let you know me and Jeff are meeting with someone who reached out to him about some potential new business. I will keep you posted."

"Awesome bud, please do."

I got up, fist-bumped, and left his office. I was starting to feel justified with how I had handled the situation with Alec. I question my judgment so much. Being an expressive, borderline over-the-top emotional person, I have sometimes thought of my reactions to everything like tossing a table during an episode of 'Housewives of...' fill in the city here. Tom gave me clarity in my thought process today. It helped more than he will ever know.

I knew I needed help, my mental state was in complete shambles. If I was going to try to salvage this, another party had to be involved. Finding some sort of assistance for my psyche was not something I took lightly. After my first go around with therapy, I could tell that Alec looked at me a little differently for a while. He didn't tell me, but I came to my own conclusion that he looked at therapy of any kind as a weakness. Since I was not about to disappoint him, I took his lead to compartmentalize, suppress, and move on. It worked for almost a decade, then this happened. I was crumbling, and with the betrayal, suppression was not going to be sufficient. I chose to go with the "mental health coach" method first. Kind of "Therapy, light." My insurance coverage led me to a program that I was comfortable trying out. I was introduced to Roseanne Rosario. She was a mix of Brooklyn girl meets Penn grad. Extremely bright and positive, but I could not ignore that sometimes she sounded like the character Gloria Clemente from "White Men Can't Jump." Smart enough to be on Jeopardy but was hanging with street hustlers. I never tried to get her story, but my mind did veer off in many directions to try and figure her out. Roseanne introduced me to Cognitive Behavioral Therapy techniques. It was tailored to help with the anxiety. It focused on thoughts and feelings and the behaviors attached to them and how to recognize these to find solutions to improve the coping aspects of life. This was much different than my suppressive approach which was now completely impractical.

I was introduced to many exercises that attempted to get my borderline depression under control. I found "Progressive Muscle Relaxation" as the best way to deal with the day-to-day grind. The key to this was to tense the body's muscle groups starting with the head and moving down to the toes. Hold the tension for 3–5 seconds, release the tension, and relax the muscles for 10–15 seconds. Then tense the next muscle group and repeat this process for all the muscle groups. I started doing this 5-6 times a day. It was like a shot of adrenaline in my body. It helped to keep me from drinking myself into oblivion each day. It didn't stop the libations but did keep me from being a certifiable drunk on most days. I was meeting with Roseanne once a week, she had become some help, until the next shoe dropped. Only so many "Catch it, Check it, Change it" I can do before my mind explodes. She and the program, at least, put me into a better place as I was navigating the holidays, with the eventual purgatory of winter.

"Wake up Love, Wake up" I opened my eyes and was in a field of lilies and the sun so bright I could hardly

make out who was talking to me. "Tara? Is that you?" "Yes, it is me silly. I want you to come with me." Tara could always hang a sundress, and this was no exception. White with a hint of yellow, her flowing blond hair always took my breath away. I grabbed her hand, and we walked in the field of lilies as far as the eye could see. "Tara, why are you here?" "I am going to take care of you. I promised to always take care of you. We are almost where we need to be." I was looking off in the distance and I saw a male figure silhouetted in the bright light of the sun. As I got closer, he got more familiar, it was my father. He was so young, younger than me, he looked like his age when he first had me. "Dad?" "Yes son, how are you? I missed you." My head was spinning, my wife and my father both took my hand and were leading me through this field. I see a building that resembles a barn of some kind. "Where are we going?" They both look at me. "You will see, this is so exciting" They both spoke simultaneously. We continued to walk and as we were getting closer to the barn, the double doors came into view. They both grabbed my hands even tighter. The door opened and we walked in. As they stopped, they released my hands. The doors closed behind me and dissolved from my view. I was alone, just the light coming through the loft windows of the barn. I called for Tara and my father. Nothing. The doors flew back open and three people walked in. Two women and a man. The light was so bright. I gazed up at the loft, Tara and my father were sitting, legs hanging over and smiling. I looked back at the door. Nothing. Then a wisp of wind from the back caused me to turn around. The "Intern," looking at me like Medusa; older, uglier, with a red tint to her eyes that were trying to draw me in. The "Hamster" was at her feet, her servant. Beadie eyes, buck teeth, hair like Rod Stewart. The third was Dan Rand. Looking more like

Voldemort. Snake-like face, bald head, and black eyes that were piercing my soul. I look up at Tara and ask "What is this Tara, what is happening?" She stares at me and simply says "We own you now, Loser." She laughs...

I open my eyes and vomit on the floor next to my bed. I am going crazy. My life is falling apart, and no amount of Cognitive Therapy is going to help that. I look at the clock. "6:41 am." No need to try getting back to sleep. I roll out of bed, avoiding the pile next to it to make my way to the cleaning supplies. No better way to start the day than a horrific dream and a pile of puke before checking emails. I take about 10 minutes and do my best to clean up the mess. I grabbed my phone and I had texts from Mary, Jeff, and Tom. All seem urgent from the night before, well past work hours. Looks like I have more damage control to deal with.

Chapter 23

Mary first, "Laura is driving me fucking crazy, can we talk??" Guess what I am starting off with today? I just called and then the floodgates opened.

"I can't take it, anymore!!"

"Hi Mary, how are you today..."

"Funny... I had enough of this bitch. She is not letting me do my job and she continuously trashes every employee in this company."

"Who in particular?"

"Tom and Jeff, all the time. You know Jeff does all this 'on the side' stuff? She tells me Dan is not happy with any of it."

"I know Jeff has his side gigs, never affected his job before. Didn't bother me or Alec."

"Yeah, we all have side stuff, that is the nature of the business. What the hell??"

"I think Dan is a little more paranoid than we are used to."

"Tired of it, TIRED OF IT! I just want to do my job and not be micromanaged. I feel their agenda, just...I don't know, never felt this way working for anyone before."

"What do you mean, Mary?"

"I am, on so many meetings with all of them. They ask me these strange questions about my life, religion, and...just not stuff you would expect on a work meeting."

"What do you want me to do?"

"Just talk to Laura, please. I can't get through to her. She has this real "henchman" thing about her. Like she is following weird orders. I don't know, seems like an Igor, something from like, Frankenstein, when I was a kid."

"Does she act kind of like a hamster?"

"On a wheel...YES!! She just turns and doesn't go anywhere. Weaselly in a way too, I get the heebie jeebies from her!"

"I will see what I can do, Mary, but fuck, I have nothing and no influence at all anymore, anywhere. I am really thinking they are about to get rid of me."

"They better not!! You are all we have. I don't trust any of these people."

"I will do what I can, Mary. I talk to Laura this afternoon."

"OK, let me know."

I get off that call and my head aches. Still have to deal with Tom and Jeff. I pour another cup of joe, take a swig, give myself a second, and call Jeff.

"Jeff, what's up?"

"Hey, I am feeling a little weird right now. Laura just texted me and seems pretty pissed off. Me and Tom made this connection with a contact person I have known for years who wants to do business with us. Laura is giving me a bunch of shit that I stepped over a line and should have just sent the information to her and not follow through!"

"Hold on...We always wanted you guys to keep your feelers up for new business. No big deal. You made the connection, and now we can move forward with it."

"Yeah, I know, but she is telling me we crossed a boundary and that I need to 'stay in my lane' or something."

"Stay in your?? What? My gawd, I can't even comment on that. This isn't the first call I got today. I will talk to Laura this afternoon."

"She told me that Tom and I have a meeting with HR tomorrow."

"HR?? for what? Trying to acquire a new business? OK, I am talking to her this afternoon. I will straighten all this crap out!"

"Thanks, man, I am getting pretty tired of all of it. Don't know how much more I can take. Tom feels the same way...Don't tell him I told you that."

I sat on this for about 6 hours. Had enough and made the call to the "hamster."

"Hey there Aeron, how's it goin'?"

"Hi Laura, fine, can we talk about what you are doing with Mary and some of the other employees?"

"Sure, what's the problem?"

"These people are pretty upset about how you are talking to them, treating them, and making them uncomfortable about you and other employees as well."

"I don't know how to feel about that, Aeron?"

"Can I just lay it out to you? When I ran operations for this company, I let our people do what they did and stayed out of the way. That is why I hired them. We have a bunch of incredibly talented people working for us."

"Sure, but I have a job to do too, and I know what I am doing. Most of these people are idiots about the technology and portals we are using, and I don't understand."

"Laura. Stop! We are not an IT-centric company; we are hands-on customer service based."

"Not anymore, I saw how Alec did things. 'Post It notes,' 'spreadsheets,' and 'chicken scratch.' We are cleaning all this garbage up."

"That 'garbage,' as you put it, made us damn successful for about a quarter century."

"Well, I am operations, and you are staffing, and let's just leave it at that."

"Laura, yeah, I am staffing, and the staff is pretty pissed off with what you are doing."

"Like what?"

"First off, Mary has a marketing degree and has been running her accounts, as is, for over 2 years. You come in and undercut everything with the clients. Just leave her alone. Jeff and Tom are keeping feelers out for new business, and you get HR involved to reprimand them? This is not good."

"Well, change is difficult sometimes. They need to start doing things the way I want and what Dan's vision is."

"Help me out with that! Dan doesn't seem to want to talk to me all that much. What the hell is the vision of this company?"

"You see on the weekly check-ins with HR. Commit to your work and be uncomfortable, the best-laid plans will then be established."

"Laura, with all due respect, I don't even know what that means."

"I think it is pretty self-explanatory, Aeron. Be uncomfortable, don't do the same thing, suffer a little and everything good happens after that."

"So, you are going to just keep doing what you are doing here?"

"Of course, that is what Dan pays me to do."

I got off the phone feeling, again, we were going around in circles. The hamster on the wheel. Not hearing me at all. The company vision wasn't sitting well. I despise change. I like doing the same thing every day. Being predictable. Setting precedent. Knowing where you stand personally and with others. I built a career by being consistent, and the last 5 months of my life and everything around me was anything but. I had to try to reason with someone before I attempted to get answers for my employees. I keep saying "My." They are not mine anymore. The realization continues to be settling in. A wave of sadness comes over me. I need to meditate or drink. Probably both. I do. Not much of the former and too much of the latter. Passing out on the couch again, another dream starts.

"Do you 'Aeron Michael' take thee 'Tara Michelle' to be your wedded wife, to have and to hold till death do you part." "I do." "Do you 'Tara Michelle' take thee 'Aeron Michael' to be your wedded husband, to have and to hold till death do you part." "I do." "You may kiss the bride." I kiss and hold her, her hands on my face as she tells me "Polar Bears" and smiles. Our inside word of love and sweetness. We walk down the aisle, all our friends clapping, at the end of the aisle I see the mist start, we keep walking, and she holds my hand even tighter. The mist gets thicker, and I cannot see a thing, as I turn to her, I cannot see her face any longer, I need to see her face. I look down at my hand and it

is empty. I look up, blink and the mist is gone. I am alone in a field. I begin to scream "Tara!!!! Tara!!!" No response. I feel the tears filling my eyes. I fall to my knees, "Tara!!! Tara!!! Where are you? I need you so much, please." Nothing.

My eyes open. I peed my pants again. I sit up, the hangover punches me back on the couch pillow. Clock. "2:36 am." I began to cry. I don't know what to do anymore. I drift back off, wishing for no more nightmares tonight.

Chapter 24

I am desperate. I need to make a call to the "intern." The "hamster" is a lost cause. If I have any chance of making any headway, I must talk to Ali, not as the "intern" but as a human being. She must know at least where this is all going. I am running out of answers. I emailed her, we set up a call right away for 10:00 am. I grab a PBR out of the fridge and take a shot of tequila. This hangover has to go. I need to be as clearheaded as possible. This won't be easy. I clicked on the Zoom link at 10:01 am, I wanted her to wait for a minute, for once.

"Hi Ali, good morning."

"Hey Aeron, I just want to let you know I have another call at 10:30."

"That is fine, I will keep this brief if I can." The shot and beer were hitting me quickly. "I am really concerned about what is happening right now. I have never seen morale this low."

"What do you mean?"

"Morale, Ali, something very important to me. I have employee after employee reaching out to me about how they are being treated, how they do the job asked of them, and just optics, basic optics."

"I don't understand. I haven't heard any of this."

"Well, I do, daily, by multiple people. Doesn't Laura mention any of this to you?"

"We talk every day, she is doing a great job."

"Ali, can you do me a favor and stop patting your-self and your people on the back? You need to realize what is going on here. You are not doing anything to nur-ture employee or client relations at all. You care more about the back office than the front."

"What does that mean?"

"Ali, you have been focusing on the portals, the systems, the IT drives and ignoring what actually matters. The "clients" and "employees." Me and Alec may have run our systems with paper clips and rubber bands, but I guarantee you everyone got paid, bills were covered, and the damn employees and clients were happy."

"Look Aeron, there is only one Alec and I get it. You worship the man, but we just do things differently, you need to get that through your head. We know what we are doing. Dan has the vision, and we are going to follow it. Commit to your work and be uncomfortable, the best-laid plans will then be established."

"Save it, Ali, Laura already told me that yester-day."

"You better start to believe in that, it is the expec-tation of all of us."

"Yeah, I know. What do you want me to do from here."

"Your job, please. I need to get on this other call. We can connect next week."

"OK, Ali, Thanks."

She dropped off and I headed to grab another double shot and PBR. I have nothing to go back to my employees with. Shut down twice by two incompetents! What kind of leader and business owner is Dan if he puts the power in these women's hands? I just don't understand. Bottoms up, drunk before 10:30, and still no breakfast.

I avoid phone calls the rest of the day. I sit in my office. I glance out the window to see the cold rain falling. I decided to just continue to torture myself more, to own all of it. The Winter purgatory has taken over my life now. I have nothing to give, just want to fall asleep, but if I do, I will be helpless to another dream, no — nightmare. I have lost count of the drinks other than the empties sitting on the coffee table with a shot glass that has had a full workout today. This is my mental health day. Time to put my misery to bed. I stumbled to the kitchen, grabbed the half-empty tequila bottle, no bother measuring, and finished the whole thing. Crawl to the couch and out. It is 2:30 pm.

"Aeron my love, wake up, we have a beautiful day ahead." Tara is straddling me. Her beautiful skin and smell I can taste and devour. I rub her, from her traps down her back and butt. I am still sleepy-eyed but feel a smile on my face as I look at her above me. Her blond hair capturing the light through the window, blue eyes that I could dive into. Love all around me. "Come on sleepyhead, make love to me, and let's go. I don't want to waste this amazing day without you." I roll her over, look deep into her eyes, both our bodies quivered together. I touch her cheek with mine, kiss her on the neck, and see the goosebumps. "Stop, you are tickling me, silly. I love you so much, Aeron." I hold her closer; she wraps her legs around me like a python. "Tara, you are everything to me. I want to...."

The phone goes off and I am pulled out of the dream. "Amber Alert!" ah geez! Oh shit! My fucking head is about to explode! Only 8:15 pm. I am a fucking mess!

Grab a glass of water, make my way to bed, and hope I don't think, dream, or do anything else other than sleep or die.

Chapter 25

I wake up the next morning, check emails and see one from the intern.

Thanks for the talk yesterday. I will take your recommendations into consideration. Please remember that for the sake of the company and employees, we expect you to buy into what the vision is. It is best for everyone.

Thanks? I don't respond. Less than an hour later, I received a company form letter email. It is announced that Vivant is no longer a company. Comptor is now the main body controlling all Vivant accounts. No use of the Vivant name will be accepted going forward. It is all gone now. No longer exists.

I cannot believe Alec allowed his legacy and life's work to be completely eliminated in less than six months. A great lesson about how much of a fraud he is. All the sacrifice for nothing. I could never have done that in any scenario. I was instructed to change everything with business correspondence. I was told to go into my LinkedIn and change my entire profile. I was so exhausted, I didn't care and did what they asked.

Although, what followed really took me down hard. I have made a point for years to turn away or connect with anything Tara has or is doing. After getting several notifications "Congratulating me" on my role with

Comptor. I made the mistake of clicking on the notifications tab. There she was. Her updated profile pic was staring at me, and Goddamn, did she look good. What happened next is what I vowed not to do, but I still clicked on her profile. It all flooded in. I saw her life right before me. No speculation anymore, the reality was right there. It was crushing.

She was doing everything we talked about. She started her own consulting company... What I always hoped she would do. She also started her own pet-sitting business... That was the worst. When she left me, she took our dog with her. That was the biggest mistake I made, not fighting for our "baby." I am sure Buffy loves to have all those dogs to play with. Years earlier, after we adopted Buffy, we had a conversation over dinner and drinks about how amazing it would be to take care of these animals. This was our way out of the rat race, and we were going to do it together. Now, she did it. On her own. Without me. I am not angry. I am proud of her. Not surprised at all. This is Tara. This is the woman I loved. Driven, focused, and gets shit done. That's my girl... Well, not my girl anymore. Why? I never wanted or needed to know.

I see my life now. Dead ends all around. I am nothing. A cog, no identity, nothing but a paycheck. Tara still inspires me, while I am nothing to her. I will never look at that profile again. I am smart enough to know what I don't need to know. That lesson was loud and clear. I did learn, unfortunately, that I am nowhere near getting over her. It may be worse now than ever.

I had another session with the mental health coach. Roseanne is very positive, almost too positive. "Think of Aeron, take care of Aeron, catch it, check it, change it." She makes me feel better for about two hours, and then it tails off. I want a magic bullet of solace that does not exist. My coping is more self-destructive than self-enhancement. I continue to receive texts and phone calls from employees. "They are messing with my pay," "What is this non-compete?" "I don't understand the 'At Will' in the employment agreement," "The handbook is ridiculous." "Aeron, help, please." I read them, I listen to them, and I can do nothing to help any of them. I have done just about everything other than scream and throw tantrums. I am irrelevant. My helplessness has put me in a position where I am almost assured that I will be let go. I have no protection. No respect or confidence that I can figure any of this out.

My biggest problem is loyalty. I am obsessed with being loyal. It has cost me on every level of my life. Family, friends, colleagues, and in my relationships with women. If only I could have that same loyalty from others. I gave my father love, money, and my future. He took all of it and walked out. Only to come back when it was convenient to use me over and over until he mercifully died of Covid during the pandemic. I took the chance with Tara, but that failed. My judgment again was just a bit off. How did I not realize that Tara was never looking for forever? She got caught up in my passion for her and went along for the ride until she was done with it. That was my ultimate miscalculation. I wouldn't trade it, but I wish it was with someone else. Alec, my last chance. How could he do this to me too? I encapsulated all my pain to give it to him to take care of. In return, I gave my life to his company. How much therapy do I need now? Immeasurable. Still so much to flesh out.

Thinking during another pity party, I have come to a bit of an epiphany. I am not looking at necessarily happiness, but reality. Being happy is a fleeting thing, but understanding the reality of what all is about has so much more fulfillment. That is why "Living your best life" is the gaslighting statement of this generation. The ultimate façade. I don't want that. I can live with the harshness of life; I don't want the mirage of what could be or is not real. Life is about pain, heartache, and finding a few glimpses and shreds of good times. I am OK with that. I just need to be able to accept that honestly, to look for a future and not the past anymore. That is a decaying car-cass that I keep going back to, which continues to stink up my life. If I learn a lesson from Tara, she is always future-focused. She never dwelled on or reminisced about the past. It was good and done. Leave it there. I har-vested the past, tilled it, and tried to keep it alive. That is my problem. She knew better. I need to get there. Let go. Our time together is a corpse, shell, nothing. Dead. Gone. Not worth the time or even a eulogy. Can I get there? One step, one crisis at a time.

I spent the next three Thursday meetings with the "intern" and the "hamster," who were half-withdrawn. Mandatory shot before getting on the calls. Barely offer-ing anything constructive. Drifting off into any other place than this meeting. Using enough business speak to get through the 30 minutes. The empty feeling of having no impact and no ability to make any sort of difference, can take its toll. I got a text from Jeff. "Can we talk? This is urgent!" I called him right away.

"What is going on, Jeff?"

"Bob Willogos reached out to me today. He wants to talk to you."

Bob Willogos is the president of Tidal Property. We run accounts in five of his buildings. To say he is our bread and butter is an understatement.

"That sounds fine. Why does he want to talk to me?"

"He has had it with Comptor."

"You mean he has had it with Ali and Laura."

"Yeah, and Dan, too."

"So, when does he want to talk?"

"Can you come down tomorrow? He wants to talk in person."

"10 am, good?"

"Yeah, I will let him know."

I sat back and thought about this. "Done with Comptor?" This was Alec's account even before I started working with him. This was the foundation of everything we built and stood for. Bob wanting to talk to me, especially without Alec. This will be very interesting.

Chapter 26

I woke up for the first time with some purpose, in what seemed like weeks. A president of an account that I nurtured, wants to talk to me directly. I dress in dark slacks, a white shirt, and a black tie. I want to represent myself in the meeting, not the company. Carry myself as if I was the president. I have met with Bob dozens of times over the years, but this will be the first time without Alec. I walk into his office, and I see Bob, his secretary, and Jeff sitting at a long 20-foot conference table. They are closer to the window. This room is on the 18th floor and has a beautiful view of the city. It sets a very good mood for the conversation. We shake hands and get started.

"What are you dressed so sharp for? I hope it wasn't for me." We all chuckled.

"I have to clean myself up sometimes, Bob. What's on your mind?"

"We are getting rid of Comptor, and I wanted to talk to you. Jeff has let me know that you have a severely diminished role with the company now. Is Alec involved at all anymore?"

"No, he isn't, and actually, we are not talking. Probably the relationship is over."

"This is odd, very odd. I have known Alec for almost 25 years, and I didn't expect he would handle his business like this. Can you shed any light on that?"

"I wish I could, Bob. He just feels he sold his company to the right people."

"How do you feel about that?"

"Honestly, Bob. This is a clusterfuck right now. The two idiots above me are inept, inexperienced, and have absolutely no clue how to run operations for a company."

"What is their experience level?"

"Ali has none, and Laura has been handling on-site operations for barely a year."

"How long have you handled operations?"

"Almost 20 years."

"That is nuts."

"Bob, give me specifics of what you are dealing with. They don't bother briefing me on anything."

"Well, first, they came in and wanted me to rip up our current contract and negotiate a new one, claiming that because of the merger and a new insurance company, they are doing this with all the accounts. Sorry, we don't negotiate with 'terrorists.' They were telling me I had to do this. No way."

"My god, that is by far the stupidest thing I have ever heard. I know this contract isn't up for about 18 more months."

"Forget that. Our lawyers are working on getting out in the next 90 days. Our contract was with you, not these bozos."

"Have you talked to Dan?"

"No, and this is the fucked-up thing, excuse my French. When we reached out to him, he deferred this back to Ali Howard. When I want to talk to the president, that should be a signal. This is why I wanted to talk to you."

"OK, and you said 'first,' so what else?"

"This is why I wanted Jeff here. He is being threatened if he doesn't sign this non-compete, they are going to fire him."

"I have been getting a lot of pushback on that one. I deferred to an attorney when they sprung it on me."

"Well, that isn't happening. Jeff isn't signing anything."

"I agree. What is going on here defies reality."

"I wanted to ask you, do you have any influence on any decisions?"

"No. not anymore."

"OK, I had a feeling from what Jeff has been telling me."

"Bob, if you can get out, do it. I just don't know how I can help you. I have been neutered about as much as anyone could be."

"Like I said, we are looking at the clauses. Can you shed any light on that?"

"Well, when we put the Tidal contracts together, there was a 90-day out for extreme neglect, but I do not know how that would work now with the contract being passed from one company to the other."

Bob's secretary gets a text and asks if she could leave the room. Less than 30 seconds later, she rushes back in with one of Tidal's lawyers. The lawyer looks absolutely stunned.

Bob speaks, "John, what the hell. You look like you've seen a ghost."

"Bob, we just went through this contract, and there was an addendum sent on July 5th from Vivant with the monthly invoice that was signed by one of our officers waiving the 90 days out and leaving the contract open for negotiation by the new owners." The lawyer, John Walker, his voice cracking, is about to have a meltdown.

"Let me see that." Bob looks intently at the papers and at the signature.

"Mother F... Alec put this in with the invoice, and Pat in accounting signed it. It is obvious he was trying to sneak something under the radar, and we didn't double-check it. We paid the damn thing before we ever knew about the merger. Is this for all five accounts?"

"Yes, it is, Bob." John said sheepishly.

"Holy shit. This has never happened with any vendor account before. I have no idea what we are going to do with this now. Aeron, can you fucking tell me anything about what Alec was thinking!!" Bob raised his voice like I had never heard before.

"Bob, he didn't say a word to me until the night before the papers were signed. I was left in the dark with everything."

"All right, we are going to try and figure something out here. I can't work with this company. You know that, right?"

"Yeah, Bob, you gotta get out of this."

"You want to take this over, Aeron? When we get rid of these bastards, you want this account?"

"You know, Bob. I don't know. I don't know if I want this anymore, but if you can get all of it worked out, we can talk."

"OK, Thanks for the time. I have to get together with the lawyers this afternoon. Just look out for Jeff, I don't trust these fuckers as far as I can throw 'em."

"I will, Bob, don't worry about that."

I left the conference room with Jeff. We were silent on the elevator, got back to the second floor and to his office. I think we were both figuring out who would speak first. I made the move.

"Jeff, how you holding up?"

"Aeron, I had to hire an attorney to help me with this non-compete. You know my social media influence and the other side projects I do. They want me to give it all up, or if I leave the company, I can't do anything for a year."

"Yeah, they tried this with me, too. I got the non-compete last week. I have an attorney friend advising me. She doesn't think this is enforceable. We both believe there is a lot of paranoia going on internally. It looks to me that Dan takes everything in his business personally. Good leaders know how to separate the business from the personal. I don't get it. I have absolutely no relationship with the guy. He uses Ali and Laura as his buffer. Strange, because those two morons couldn't punch themselves out of a paper bag."

"Well, I need this to go away. The stress is taking its toll on me. Thank God, Bob is fighting for me. If I didn't have him, I wouldn't know what to do."

"You're fortunate, Jeff. I have no one looking out for me now."

"Do you think they are going to fire you?"

"Maybe... Probably."

"Sorry, man."

"I will be fine, bud. I am always fine."

We fist-bumped, and I headed out. I left the building and decided to go on a very long walk. Walk to nowhere but needed something to clear the head, after all that. It didn't work. Finished out the day and headed back home. That's where the booze is.

Chapter 27

I woke up the next morning glad I did not have a hangover or nightmare. Two for two, to start the day. I am still contemplating the meeting from the day before. Alec manipulated a company and a man who had taken care of him for over two decades. "How does he sleep at night?" I was stunned, but not anymore. Every pass I could give him is gone now. He lied to everyone. I am just one of many. Alec didn't just betray me; he did this to all our employees, clients, and liaisons with whom he built relationships throughout his whole career. Now, his legacy does not exist anymore. Vivant is no longer a company. Gone. I try to wrap my head around one thing, then must move on to another. "How much longer before everything is gone?" I sit at my desk with no motivation, "Do they just need to put me out of my misery?" I look at the clock, it's 9:37 am. "Too early for a drink, or is it?"

I check my email, the "intern" without anyone else on the note.

Good morning. I have a shareholder meeting on Thursday. Can we move the normal Thursday meeting to Wednesday at 2:30?

I responded with a yes. I am a little curious that the "hamster" was not on the reschedule. I will get the story from her. After making my usual daily rounds, finishing around 4:30 pm, the end of the business call to the "hamster."

"Hey, Laura."

"Hey."

"Before we get into it, I see that Ali is changing our meeting this week. Are you going to be on the call with us?"

"Oh No, Me and Alec have a new business meeting at that time. No biggie."

"You and Alec? Interesting coincidence."

"Oh yeah, we set this up a few weeks ago."

"Really, we haven't talked about that at all in our dailies."

"Just slipped my mind."

We went through the traditional daily checklist and ended the call. Something just didn't feel right about that.

I get up for a normal Wednesday of checking emails, catching up on calls, and then heading out to meet with staff. I want to get a solid day in before speaking to Ali that afternoon. I have little feeling, not because of anything, just a lack of a concrete agenda. My last stop is with a manager original to Comptor who I had never met in person before. Sal is a kid I had heard about a lot but seen only in a few Zooms. He looked beaten down. He expressed some of his frustrations with leadership, especially the relationships with Laura and Ali. I told him I would work hard to try to help make it better. I didn't believe my own words. Just lip service to make him feel at ease that afternoon. I made my way back to the office to prepare for what would be another dead-end call with the "intern."

I got back to my home office and pulled up the call invite. Still just Ali and me. I had twenty minutes. I was on edge, as I am, every time I spoke to this kid. I poured a shot of Avion Tequila and prepared some salt, lime, and a Coors light chaser. The clock was 2:18 pm, and there was plenty of time to let this kick in before dealing with her. I took down the shot and chased, feeling disgusted. I headed up to the office. Set myself in front of my screen. I decided to get on a little late. Gamesmanship, petty, I know. I pulled myself in at 2:32 pm. There was Ali, the "intern," the unquestioned leader of this ship, accompanied by the HR manager. She was sly. HR wasn't on the invite, but as soon as I saw both of their faces, I knew I was in trouble, it was over.

"Hi Aeron, this is a difficult moment right now. I wanted to tell you first off how hard this is, but we have given you six months, and it is not working out. We are going to let you go today."

I was sitting stunned, yet not surprised. I couldn't say a word as Ali kept going.

"We know this has to be shocking and sorta crazy for you after all this time, but we decided that this was best for all parties."

I was staring at the HR manager, who looked like she would rather be at a funeral than this. Zoom calls take the courage out of a firing. I spent years preparing to deal with someone face to face, in person, to tell them, "Yeah, you aren't cutting it. You don't have to go home, but you ain't working here anymore." Kidding aside. Alec and I labored over firings more than anything else. We always did them together, in person, showing the respect of the president and operation director, looking the man or woman in the eye and telling them that this wasn't working anymore. What did I get? A Zoom call, the clueless, inept and worthless "intern" giving a little lip service and then telling me, "I am going to pass the rest of this off to HR."

She dropped me off without an acknowledgment that I am a human being. I looked at the HR director and told her, as resigned as I could be, "I am not going to make this hard for you. I know what you are doing now. Let's just finish this and go on with the day." She was appreciative. It wasn't her fault. I had a feeling that this ruined her day in some way, too. Less than 8 minutes, 2:40 pm, and we were done. It didn't take another 10 minutes before my phone went off. Jeff, Tom, Mary, and several other employees with the same notable gasp. "Oh my God!" Jeff sent me a screenshot of the email to the employees, "*Breaking News—Termination of Employee*" The body was a bunch of bullshit corporate speak, but what I deciphered from it was more of, shape up folks, or you are next. I was a little smarter than some people gave me credit for. I was an example and knew it was coming. I finished the bottle of tequila that night, certainly more, I am sure, but I couldn't remember.

Chapter 28

Another hangover woke me up. The decision between coffee and liquor was a little closer than I was comfortable with. My life has changed in every possible way. I expected the next week to be very difficult. I will wake up on Monday morning for the first time without the Monday anxiety. I will also rise without anything of substance to do, which is not exactly a good thing for me either. The pandemic taught me so much about "manufacturing" moments. Those lessons will help a lot in this transition.

I have not felt the real emotions yet. I am sure there is a good cry, panic attack waiting out there somewhere. I have to come to the reality that my career is over. Everything I worked on for over 20 years is gone and will never come back. How it all ended is something else I will have to rectify in my mind. No celebration, no party, no appreciation. I was kicked out the door. Thrown on the side of the road, like a piece of trash. How I was treated over those six months was dreadful. Maybe there is a book in that. I now sit in this empty house with no job, no love, no friends, and no future. It is 8:06 am, and drinks sound good. I have no job and nothing to do. Why the hell not?

I started the bender. I played Marilyn Manson on a loop, "We've only reached the third day of a seven-day binge. I honestly see your name disintegrated from my lips." That day went by in a flash. I pass out.

"Baby Boy, wake up. I want to dance." Tara was such a free spirit to only me. I was special. She was able to open up to me like she couldn't to anyone else. No one made me feel so good, like I was put on this earth to be just for her. We could dance in the moonlight or our living room... "Play our song, baby. I want you so much." I knew our song, cheesy and beautiful. She was my domino. "I am feeling sexy and free, like glitters raining on me... You're like a shot of pure gold, and I think I'm 'bout to explode." No one could dance like Tara. I know I am in a dream. I am drunk in ecstasy or REM sleep and loving every second of this. "Don't you know, you're spinning me out of control?" She does three beautiful twirls in front of me, and she gives me the look. We both know the look. "We can do this all night, damn this love is skintight. Baby, come on. Oooh ooh ooh ooh." She grabs and pulls me in, genitals first. We feel it, and I am in no better place in the world. "Rock my world until the sunlight. Make this dream like I've never known." I kiss her hard like it is the first time. "Dirty Dancing in the Moonlight, take me down like I'm a Domino." We dance, we sing, we feel love that we have never known before. "You got me losing my mind, my heart beat out of time." She knew every word and looked at me as such. We make love all night. Inside the house, in the yard, experiment everywhere. She wants me, I oblige, I want her, she obliges. It is perfect, and I never want it to end. She is my Domino. The most beautiful woman in the world wants me. I know I am not worthy, but I lap it all up. This is my time, my lottery. Tara is my prize. Every second is a spotlight. "I love you so much, Tara... Tara... Tara, where are you?" Everything gets fuzzy, the light, the goddamn light.

I awake. The sun is shining through the living room window, and I again passed out on the couch. I pissed my pants again. Maybe something else in there, too. Who the hell knows? My first night after being fired. I did a bang-up job of dealing with the situation.

I do not even know how to start a new day. I have never been unemployed, always had a purpose, something to do. To have the plugged pull, I struggle to start even what would be the most menial of tasks. Should I take a shower and get dressed? What's the point? I check my email, and the HR director sent me my *"Notice of Dismissal"* letter and some legal doc confirming my last check and severance. It is real if it is in black and white. Time for a drink. I have no place to go and ain't got shit to do. I pretty much cleaned out the house that day of any alcohol. Thankfully, I had not purchased much in a while, or I may be getting my stomach pumped. By 2:00 pm, I am half-dressed, barely able to get out of bed. Didn't even bother settling in the living room. The iPhone handles all my music choices as I listen to any and every heartbreak song I can find. I drift off to "Landslide" by Stevie Nicks, the version she dedicated to "Daddy."

"Son, son, we need to talk." "Sure, Pop, what's on your mind?" He was sitting in the kitchen. I walked in, getting ready to head off to school; I was about 17 years old. So much more innocence and hope for life. I was with the person I loved and admired the most. My dad was my hero, and I hung on to just about anything he said. He had been taking care of the money I had been making over the last two years, and all I needed to do was pick a college and keep my grades up. It was hard, but I knew Pop was taking care of everything for me.

"Aeron..." "Hold on, Pop, I want to show you this. I may be able to get a scholarship to attend the state. My counselor is telling me if I have enough for the first semester, she thinks I can get the next three semesters paid for. Which means we are set until junior year. Here is the paperwork we need to fill out for this." "That is great, Aeron, I will look at it later. Listen, I have something to tell you." He paused, and I sat down. He had a look on his face that was not like him. My dad was the coolest guy in town. Everyone loved him, especially my mom. He was funny, whip-smart, and had all the answers. I was worried about him. What could be wrong? "Aeron, the money is gone." "What do you mean gone, Pop? It is like $16,000. I gave up the last two summers and have been working weekends for what feels like months now." "It is gone. I will get it back, but it is gone now." He got up from his chair and threw his coffee cup in the sink, breaking instantly. "Pop, what does this mean?" "What do you think it means, Aeron!! You can't go to college right now, OK? No scholarship, no State, nothing. I need time to figure this out." I got out of my seat, trying not to hyperventilate, "Pop, it will be OK. You will figure it out. You always do." "Yeah, kiddo, I always do. Just give me some time, Ok?" I walk over and hug him, "It will be fine, Pop."

The mist returns, and I am again alone, trying to make my way through. "Pop, where are you, Mom? Mom, what is going on?" I come to a door; the mist disappears. I open the door, and it is only my Mom in the room, sitting at a table with a bottle of Vodka and a pistol, "You bastard, you left me. You destroyed your son's life, and there is nothing I can do to fix it. I hope you are happy." She is speaking to no one but herself. As she looks up and sees me at the door, *tears roll down her cheeks. She picks up the pistol and says, "I am sorry," and pulls the trigger.*

I vomit on myself, still half asleep, roll over to the other side of the bed, and cry in the fetal position. I have lost everything and have no control of anything anymore.

Chapter 29

I attempt to gather myself over the next few days. The struggle to stay sane becomes more challenging than ever. I will lose my insurance at the end of the week. I have one more session with Roseanne, and I need to make the most of it. She is no miracle worker, but she is all I have right now. I need to try to find some path out. I pulled myself together, and we met at 11 am on a Friday.

I get on the video call, and I try to put together notes, but that really doesn't get me anywhere. Roseanne pops on.

"Hi, Aeron. How are you? It's good to see you."

"Roseanne, how are you doing today?"

"Great, Great, I see you took care of the assignments I gave you."

"Yeah, the 3 C's, relaxation exercises, avoidance actions, behavioral experiments, got it." Even though I was completely falling apart, I am wired to complete assigned tasks. It is just my default.

"So, what is happening this week?"

"Well, Roseanne, I got fired a few days ago, and this is the last day I have insurance coverage with my company, so I have a feeling we have a lot to go through in a short period of time."

"Oh god, I am sorry, Aeron. Umm, I will take this in another direction if you like. What can I do to help?"

"Quite frankly, I am pretty scared right now. I have been drinking myself to sickness, and my dreams are about to drive me insane. I need to know if I should be getting real help here or not."

"OK... As we both discussed, I am a mental health coach and not a licensed therapist, but I do know enough to be able to ask you some questions and see if you need to get into real hardcore therapy."

"That sounds good, fire away."

"Do you cry for no reason?"

"Yes."

"Are you thinking negatively about yourself and life in general?"

"Yes."

"Do you have unhealthy habits?"

"Like drinking every day to excess?"

"That would be one."

"Well, then, yes."

"Do you feel like your emotions are controlling you?"

"What do you mean by that?"

"Are you irritable, lashing out, feeling out of control with day-to-day things, not able to cope with life?"

"Yes, to all of that."

"Final question, are you suicidal?"

I pause long and hard before answering, "No, not yet."

"Not yet? So that is on the table, then?"

"No, not yet. I guess I will know if or when that ever arrives."

"Aeron, I am worried. You are going out on your own with no resources or ability to get help of any kind."

"That is what this looks like, doesn't it?"

"Yes, and to give you my take on this, you desperately need therapy."

"Winner, winner, boss. Sorry to be cynical. You didn't have to tell me that, I already know, but there is nothing I can do. I just wanted to hear from a professional that I need help. Just because I am going crazy doesn't mean I am completely insane."

"I don't think you are crazy or insane, Aeron. You are just going through a really bad time here. I have a feeling that you have a lot more to unpack than just this job situation."

"You are on to something there, too, Roseanne. So, what do I do as a middle-aged unemployed guy in this climate?"

"I really can't answer that question, but I do recommend that you find some insurance as quickly as possible and meet with someone. It is vital because you are slipping into a bad place."

"This is all new to me, and I guess I have some research to do."

"Look, Aeron, you can text or email me anytime. You have been a great student over the last six weeks of this program. You are burnt out and were given some messed up circumstances. All is not lost, but I don't feel you can fix this on your own."

"Well, I do believe you are right. I appreciate you being available for me. I will not bother you unless absolutely necessary. I know we have to end this session, Roseanne. I appreciate you getting out of your comfort zone to do some quick evaluation. You have been great. Take care of yourself."

"Aeron, you too. Please get some help, it is really important. All the best."

She drops off the call. I take a swig of my vodka tonic. I am going to miss her; she is a good egg. Looks like I do check all the nutso boxes, but at least I am not suicidal yet. Let's see how long that lasts.

Chapter 30

I take a few days to sober up to evaluate my life. The work colleagues' calls start to dry up. I think I am getting a toothache that, without insurance, I can't deal with. I am of prime age for a heart attack, and if I play my cards right, I am assured of being homeless within the next 12-18 months. I ask myself a question, "I am sober, because?" I like to think that I choose to drink, 'cause I do not have a reason not to. The pitiful side of me continues to ask, "Why did this happen?" While the rational side just tells me, "Why not?" I am trying to find a way to cope without going straight to the bottle again.

So I decided to explore YouTube to try to find some answers. After a bunch of searches for "Depression Symptoms," "Therapy," and "Dealing with Job Loss," I stumbled onto a series of videos with an LMFT, the acronym for Licensed Marriage and Family Therapist, when I saw the blond-hair, blue eyes, and facial structure, all I see is Tara. I spent the next few hours listening to her, sounding eerily like Roseanne but looking so much like my ex-wife. One video stood out to me, and it wasn't just that the therapist was wearing a blue V-neck sweater that looked like something that would be in Tara's closet. She also wore a necklace that looked like a gift from our fifth wedding anniversary. She discussed something called Dysthymia, or for dummies like me, "High Functioning Depression." This is a low-grade depression that lasts most days for at least two years. Well, my marriage began to collapse almost four years ago, so that checks. She tells me it is something that hangs around continuously, and feels like a dull ache in the psyche.

After rattling off about bunch of symptoms, like appetite issues, insomnia, fatigue, concentration problems, and hopelessness, she states something right after that hits me like a thunderbolt. This disorder can make someone feel exhausted and frustrated in dealing with their situation in life. That has been my last six months, probably a lot more before that. The difference was I had Alec prior to convincing me to compartmentalize and suppress. The therapist addresses the unhealthy coping skills, and that is the crux of the problem. Without my only line of support. Not having Alec to take care of me on a day-to-day basis and being alone. Not having my employees to feed off or them feeding off me. I turn to what I know: booze and blackout.

Anxiety and depression are close friends, as I am finding out. They both love hanging out with me, especially when I am dwelling in the cesspool of my past. Lack of control in life exasperates all of it. She cheerfully finished each video, and this one included "Be your own advocate." I don't know what that means. I shut it down and realized I needed therapy that I could not acquire. I choose to finish my day, as I have been, for most of the last few weeks, drunk. I again pass out, but at least I am in night clothes this time.

"I need you. I need you. I need you. I need you." I hear this over and over. Different voices saying it each time. Some females, some males, some more familiar than

others. I am walking down another long hallway, dark, mist doors, like so many of the other dreams. I am bracing myself because I have been here before. I know I am dreaming and just want to wake up. I can't. I keep walking. I ran into a door, it opens. "I need you," it is Mom. Door closes. It opens again. "I need you," It is Dad. It closes. Opens "I need you," the "intern," and the "hamster," they laugh and slam the door. Opens, "I need you." Alec flips me off and closes the door. I am covering my ears and closing my eyes "STOPPP, PLEASE STOPPP!!!" I wait for a minute. When I open my eyes, the hallway is lighted, and the mist is gone. Tara is standing in front of me, wearing the blue V-neck sweater and necklace. She smiles, "I need you," she reaches for me, and the floor opens. I fall...

My eyes open, I am on my back. I think I jerked so hard I pulled something. I investigate; no puke and no piss, so I made it out of this one unscathed. I turn over and begin to cry. This is becoming a ritual. I do not want to get out of bed. I hurt all over. I am beginning to think of things that are scaring me. Do I want to be here anymore? Do I need to deal with this every night? How many more hangovers can I take? I have no one, and I don't want to burden anyone. I am turning into a pathetic old man right before my eyes. I have nothing, and I am nothing. I get up, stub my toe on the bedpost, and fall to the floor. Is that a sign?

I got a text later that day from Jeff. "Hey, they are putting your job out there now. These people suck. Seems like they are looking for primarily females to apply?" I respond, "Is that even legal?" "I don't know. I found it on a job board that focuses on female empowerment. My girlfriend showed me." "There is something so strange about the demographics of this company, Jeff."

"Yeah, like they don't want dudes or something, LOL." "Just keep me updated, bud. I am curious what direction they want to go in with this." "You bet. Are you doing OK?" "Jeff, I am still alive. I have pretty low expectations these days." "I get it. Hang it there and call me if you need to talk." "Thanks."

I do not understand why these guys only want women to work for them. Especially underqualified or not qualified at all. They are all so damn young too. I will never get any answers. My life is too fucked up to figure myself out. I cannot put a sock and shoe on today. If I broke this toe, I swear. I limp around the house, sparingly attempting to be productive. Fail. I just sit on the couch and stare at the clock. I am trying to get through the day without having a drink. 1:00 pm, 2:00 pm. Nap. 4:30 pm, 5:30 pm, 8:00 pm. I made it. Doing absolutely nothing, I go to bed. The only accomplishment of the day was not getting drunk. I hope I sleep better. No more dreams. That would be a victory. Living a life of low expectations.

I spent another week on the wagon, off the wagon. Navigating unemployment, insurance, and even looking into food stamps. My dignity had taken a vacation as well. I started to do the searches that would possibly take me over the line. "Easy Suicide Methods," "Carbon Monoxide Poisoning," "Are guns or hanging easier ways to kill yourself?" "How much alcohol will kill you?" I spend an afternoon with this, and it goes into the evening. I am somber as I look at each article and watch each video. I am waiting for an internal sign that says, "Yes, this is how we are going to do it." Fortunately, or unfortunately, the sign didn't come. I took the fortunate route today. Cannot guarantee to feel the same tomorrow. I get up and stagger to bed. Another day, still no answers, now I am running out of questions. I am in real trouble.

Chapter 31

I wake up and check emails. They are drying up as well. When you have no purpose and are not necessary for any business dealings, you find that all you receive are Telehealth Compliance, AARP membership rewards, Hello Fresh, and, of course, Sex Secrets. This morning does not seem to be worth the time to go through that. I did see some traction from my unemployment filing. A message from the low-cost insurance provider I put an application in for. I guess that is my day's work now. My body hurts, hurts all over. I cannot determine if it is a product of all the alcohol, my lack of quality sleep, my age, or a combination of it all. I need to get a place to just break the monotony. I decided to take a long walk. I have a trail about a mile from my house. I have not thought about exercise much or consistent activity in what seems like weeks. I jump in the shower, take one much longer than normal, and attempt to wash some of the gloom off. I dress in jeans, a long-sleeved T-shirt, grey mid-calf socks, and my low-top Merrill slip-on hikers. They haven't been much use in years. I hold the shoes in my hand before slipping them on. These are the shoes I wore when I and Tara climbed the Flatirons in Boulder, Colorado, the year before things started to go bad. The Rock formations are stunning to look at. They define the region. The adventure started on the Royal Arch Trail, a three-mile stretch that took us to nearly 6600 feet above sea level. It is the kind of trail that builds relationships. You cannot do this alone and get the same effect. You lean on each other, push each other, and feel the accomplishment at the top of the trail, looking over the city of Boulder. We could faintly see the city of Denver in the distance. In September, this area of the country is about as ideal as anywhere in the world. At the top, we kissed and took a selfie. We still had our love. Making our way down we had lunch and drinks on Pearl Street, the hot tub at the hotel, then went back to our room. It was the most perfect day with the most perfect person.

I get up off the couch, make sure my socks are not bunching up in the shoes, and head to the door. I make my way to the trail. This is in no way as breathtaking as Boulder, but a nice creek runs along, and the sound is very soothing. I have done a lot of thinking while walking this trail when I first moved to this area. Trying to come to terms with losing the love of my life, refocusing on what my identity would be going forward. I made my deeper commitments to Vivant and Alec on this trail. There is a waterfall about midway. I stop to look over the water, trying desperately not to break down. I am not the only person walking. A young college-age kid with his highly active dog walked by me, a couple holding hands about 10 feet from me, glancing over the same water. I look down at the shoes and stare at them for a moment. I think back again to Boulder. "Hey, mister...mister." I snap out of it and look up, "Yes, what can I do for you." It is the girl with her boyfriend. "Can you take a pic of us with the waterfall, please?" They were very cute, a couple that looked like they should be together. "Sure, no problem." She hands me her iPhone 11, and I frame the photo just right, snap three for them, and hand back the phone. "These are great. Thanks, mister." They kiss, smile then continue with the moment they are in. I sigh and start back on the hike, still having some time left to clear my head.

I got back home and checked the clock, 11:37 am. I was out for almost 2 hours. Much better use of my morning than what I have been doing. I take the shoes off. The memories are weighing on my feet. Slip on a pair of Asics Gel Nimbus I used to run in. They are always very comfortable. By habit, I check emails again. Only one, and in the subject line, I need you.   I   double-take, I need you. It can't be. Tara hasn't reached out to me in over two years. What would she want? The thought leaves my head as my eye moves to the name. Sara O'Connor. It must be some sort of solicitation. It is a Gmail account, and maybe someone just sent the wrong email. I click on it to see, about to press delete, when my curiosity or lack of anything else to do now causes me to check the email.

Hello Mr. Harmon

I am sorry to bother you. I got your private email after you were fired from some previous correspondence when the merger happened back in the summer. It is very important that I talk to you. So many things to say, but I do not want to do it in an email, I understand that you were unjustly fired by the Comptor. I work for Comptor and work closely with Dan. There is so much you need to know about what is going on here. It is wrong, and I am scared it is going to get worse. I have no one to try and help me expose all of these things. I need you. Can we please talk?

Thank You

Sara O'Connor

I am fixated on *I need you*. I read it a few more times. I leave it up on the screen and go to the kitchen for a drink. If I am going to do anything with this, I need to clear my head. I come back to break down each sentence and each word, grab my legal pad and start crafting a response. I attempt to let her down easily.

Hello Ms. O'Connor

I appreciate you reaching out to me, and I will say I am curious about the happenings at Comptor, but I am trying to move on with my life. I do not know how I can help you. I have nothing to provide to you other than what I saw in the six months before they let me go. I am not happy with how the company is being run, but it doesn't matter now. I am gone and already forgotten. Thank you. I am sure someone currently with the company would be more of a help to you.

Sincerely
Aeron.

That should take care of that. What the hell can I do to help? When I was there, I didn't matter. I was pushed aside and thrown away. I am more ready to die than to try and help anyone. I need you. I chuckle and shake my head. No one needs me. I get up from the computer and try to manage the rest of the day. I was too tired from the walk to go get any more booze, so I only had a half bottle of Barefoot Chardonnay in the fridge. I sip through that and muster up a macaroni and cheese and some turkey corn dogs for dinner. Very gourmet, if I must say so. I watch the sun go down through the living room and start to drift off. I catch myself and make my way back upstairs. I pass by my office on the way to the bedroom, and again, curiosity brings me back to the computer. I am sure there is nothing, but what the hell? I wake the computer up to the only message waiting, which is from Sara. She edited the subject. PLEASE, I need you. I plop in my chair and read the response.

Mr. Harmon, Aeron,

I want to stress to you that YOU are the only person I can turn to about anything. I did not want to put this in an email, but if this is the only way to get your attention.

I have a video that you need to see. It is Alec and Dan discussing the merger. Dan blackmailed Alec into selling his company to Comptor. I have this video. That is all I can say to you about it right now.

Please, I have to meet you. Tomorrow, if possible, this is urgent. Please.

Sara

OK, now she has my attention. I have to absorb that statement for a second. Dan blackmailed Alec into selling his company to Comptor. There is no friggin' way Alec would allow himself to be blackmailed. Alec may be an asshole, but he is such a savvy business guy he would never let himself be put in any position to be taken advantage of. I at least knew that about the man. I guess I don't really have a choice now. I responded to the email. Sara and I decided to meet at the public library about 2 miles from my house. They have a private meeting room that can be used for up to 30 minutes. I went online and reserved the room for 1:30 pm. I cannot sleep right away, thankfully, without anything to drink. I just lie in bed and play the "Don't check the clock game" that insomniacs struggle with all the time. I only did it three times: 12:48 am, 1:26 am, and 3:01 am. I fell asleep soon after that. Thankfully, for the rest of the night.

Chapter 32

I woke up around 8:15 am, pretty pleased that I got a much better sleep than I would have imagined. Grab a coffee, and try to stay busy until the meeting. I decide to walk to the library, this will get my head in the right place to kill some time, as well. The most important thing is to not think of anything that may sidetrack the task at hand. I am about to meet someone who is going to explain to me how Alec was blackmailed. I still cannot wrap my head around that, but no sense in overthinking. I head out around 10:30 am and plan to take my time on this. I don't know if I want to get involved. I am starting to enjoy my new normal of hating myself and life.

I arrive well before 11:30 and check in with the library clerk. She directs me to the room. It is very small. Enough for a round table, 2 chairs, and a tacky piece of art on the wall that looks like an Alexander Calder rip-off. I moved the table and chairs so that I would be facing Sara. I do not know this woman, so it is important to keep my personal space. I have always been cognizant of my relationships with the females in my employ. I treated them no differently than men, maybe even in a more benign way. I never wanted to be "that guy" who used his power to make women feel uncomfortable. I shake hands and never make a comment on clothes, hair, or any other feature that I would not say to a man. This helped me create great rapport and respect with my team, top to bottom. I do not know what this woman's motivation is to want to talk to me. Since she is coming from Comptor, the company that just fired me, I really want these boundaries to be heavily implied if not fully known. I decided to wait in the front lounge of the library. I pick up a People magazine dated from a year earlier, I just stare at the date on the cover and think quickly about how much different my life was a year ago. Never would have pictured I would be in this place today. Sara walked in. I knew it was her right away, 11:30 on the dot. I stood up. "Hello, Mr. Harmon. So nice to meet you." She smiled a very warm smile, and I was immediately put at ease. She is around 5'5, maybe 120 pounds, with auburn hair and blue eyes. She does not look very athletic but carries herself and her weight well. She appeared young but not as young as I would think. She smells very natural. No heavy perfume. Smells like what I would think a woman should smell like. Very modest dress. Navy blue slacks, white blouse, and slip-on black Skechers. She is carrying a computer bag over her right shoulder. "I appreciate you meeting me today, Mr. Harmon." "Please, call me Aeron." She smiles again, "OK, Aeron." I nodded to the clerk, and we headed back to the reserved room that we had for a half hour.

We both step in, and I close the door; we take our seats. She starts right away and pulls out a Dell laptop computer and a Mead spiral notebook that definitely looks like it had a good workout.

"Aeron, I want to walk you through a few things, and then I will show you the video."

"Sara, can I just ask why you reached out to me about this?"

"Because I know your role with Vivant and have an idea of the relationship you had with Alec."

"And what role was that?"

"Well, you were operations director for close to 20 years. You had worked with Vivant longer than that, I believe. I know how much Alec spoke of you and that he was discussing a handover of the company to you. He was planning to be a limited partner, and you handle all day to day."

"How do you know this?"

"I am Dan's personal secretary. I took notes in all these negotiation meetings. That is what I have in this notebook. I wasn't a part of any of the hardcore stuff, mostly just taking foundational notes that helped him work with Ali and Laura as the negotiations commenced."

"Alec spoke of me in these foundational meetings?"

"Yes, he seemed to me to be torn with what he wanted to do. Dan started working on him about 2-3 years ago. Dan was really determined and wanted Vivant desperately. I never understood why. Well, until the last few months."

"What has been going on the last few months?"

"I have uncovered a lot of things about what Comptor is doing, and it really has to stop."

"Dan is just a business guy, a dick, but just doing business nonetheless."

"No, if it was just that, I would never have reached out to you. What I have uncovered is more than business, much more."

Sara had not told me anything concrete yet, but her tone continued to get sterner and more serious.

Whatever she wanted to tell me, it was probably going to be something I needed to brace for.

"OK, Sara, fire away."

"Look, I don't want to show this to you here. Can we go back to your place and do this? I am a little paranoid."

"Why? Is someone following you?"

"No, but I have been skeeved out for the last week or so. I would rather be in a different environment."

"OK, we can go back to my house. I walked here. Can you give me a lift?"

"Umm, why don't you leave and walk to the strip mall with the Rainbow Cleaners? I will pick you up there in about 10 minutes."

"Sure, that sounds fine."

I left the room first as she started to gather her things back up. I walked out of the library and headed to Rainbow Cleaners. The strip mall was only about 2 blocks from the library, so it was an easy walk. I was getting anxious about what the next step was going to look like. I met this woman less than a half hour ago, and now she is coming to my house. She works for Dan Rand? Close to Dan but is not part of the negotiating process. Again, what does she want to do with me?

I reached the destination and waited on the sidewalk. Sara pulled up in a Red Hyundai Sonata that looked maybe a year old Florida plates. Could it be a rental? I stepped into the car, which still had a hint of a new car smell to it.

"Is this your car, Sara?"

"Yes, I drove up and got here yesterday afternoon. Dan thinks I am on a week's vacation."

"You live in Florida?"

"No, right now, I live in Berlin, Georgia. That is where Dan has his office and where he and his family live. I am from Tallahassee, Florida. Only about an hour away. My parents and two sisters live there."

"Just take a left at the light here and first right. My townhouse is at the end of the road."

"OK."

"So, where do you live in Berlin? I have never heard of that town."

"I live on his compound. A spare house next to his Church."

"His church?"

"Yes, he runs his own church on the compound, I will tell more once we get settled."

"OK, no problem."

I look out the passenger side window as the homes roll by. My head is spinning. I still haven't been told anything. Yet, I feel like the bomb is about to be dropped on me in some way. We arrive at my house and go in. I look around to see if any neighbors are watching. I have not had a woman in my house in almost three years.

I am not very pleased with my housekeeping lately. When you are a head case and borderline drunk, it doesn't make way for the happy homemaker. I scramble to tidy up the living room and make the kitchen somewhat respectable. I glance at Sara as I scramble. She is intently looking around my home. I am hypersensitive to her glances. My home is a collection of art, old pictures, posters, and sports memorabilia, sadly accumulated while I was with Tara. My office is the only place that carries any substance. Degrees, remnants of college, my computer, and other worthless work items. I asked her if she would like a drink. I am more than ready to dive into something strong. "Sorry about the look of the place. Can I get you anything? Would you like a drink?"

"What do you have?"

"She has no idea that I have been stinking drunk for days now and have more empties in the recycling than anything else in the house. I have a few options. Alcohol, or no?"

"Well, I will start with something light, but I may need something a little stronger after we talk."

"Kombucha, Seltzer or water?"

"Just a water is fine for now."

I am running low on booze, so I pour her a large glass of water from my Brita pitcher. I refrain from the Makers Mark in the cabinet for now and pour myself a glass of H2O, as well. I want to try to control my anxiety naturally as we continue our conversation. I walk into the living room with both glasses, and she already has the computer plugged in and set up on the coffee table.

"Aeron, I am going to show you something, we can talk about it after. Just give me a second to cue it up."

I sit next to her on the couch. We are inches from touching elbows. She has no concerns. She is focused completely on pulling up this video that is being pre-pared. I sit intently, and maybe the drink would have been a better idea than the water.

"OK, we are about ready. I am going to show this to you, and we will talk about it afterward."

I would have been more comfortable sitting back on the couch cushions, but something told me I had to be on the edge of my seat for this. The recording started.

"Hello, everyone, Alec, Ali, and Laura. How is everyone today?"

They all responded to Dan and were very pleasant at the outset.

"Alec, hope all is well. We are looking to get things moving forward. What are your considerations about the last meeting we had."

The "intern" chimed in. "Should I go through minutes first, Dan?"

"Not necessary, Ali."

"Dan, how is everyone? Just wanted to follow up. When we talked last week, we were looking to go to another level with the negotiations, but I have some thoughts first... I have been thinking. We have been discussing a lot over the last few years, and as much as I want to move forward, I am leaning toward keeping Vivant solvent and just having Aeron take this thing over, and I will just counsel him through everything. We are doing really well right now, and Aeron has all this covered and then some. I can still take the step back, and he can step in."

I could not believe what I was hearing. The meeting got quiet for well over a minute. I could see the "intern" and the "hamster" squirming a bit, like they knew something that Alec didn't. I moved a little closer to the screen. Sara sat nearly motionless.

"Alec, I, we appreciate that about Aeron, but to be frank, he is not a part of the plan here. You are, and I want to share some information that has come across my desk."

"Information?" Alec seemed genuinely surprised.

"I will just use one word... Kyra."

As soon as that name left Dan's lips, I saw all the blood rush out of Alec's face.

"Yes, Kyra Bacon. That name appears like it is familiar."

"Yeah, I know her." Alec's mind was in full overdrive.

"Look, Alec, let's cut through it. Kyra works for me in new business development, and she came to me a while back with news of some sort of relationship with you."

Alec was speechless, like I had never seen him before. I knew there was something wrong.

"What did she tell you, Dan?"

"Well, she is a young girl, and it took me a while to get out of her what she wanted to say, but you two have been carrying on for almost a year now."

Alec again took what was quite an inordinate amount of time before responding.

"What do you mean carrying on, Dan?"

"Alec, Kyra is saying that you have been sleeping together quite frequently for a long time."

"She is craz...." Alec stopped and paused for a moment before composing to continue the conversation. "If I denied this, it wouldn't get me anywhere, would it? By the way, can we just talk? I don't think it is appropriate to have Ali and Laura on a call with information like this?"

"No, Alec, it is very appropriate that they are on. Let's just get into what the talk is about today. We all know now that this happened. Ali, you have the pics, right?"

The "intern" pulled one up of Alec kissing this young girl probably half his age. "Yeah, Alec, we took this one outside that café in Berlin when you came down last summer."

Dan smiled and kept talking, "You two looked like you were having a great time, and we also have a video of when you two snuck off to that cabin on my property. You have some real stamina for a guy in his sixties, gotta say."

Alec appeared resigned and looked down at his desk, took a deep sigh, and responded. "What do you want?"

"Alec, we have had a great working relationship and friendship for almost a decade now. I just want you to close this deal. You have been hemming and hawing. I don't understand why. You will still be a part of this. You are the face of Vivant. Is this about Aeron Harmon? Please, he is nothing. I will keep him on. No big deal. Let's just get this thing done."

Alec was quiet again, and I could see his mind was working overtime, but he had no answer to what was happening now.

"OK, Dan, let's just finish it. Don't worry about Aeron. He will be fine with all of this. I will talk to him. He does anything I say, anyway."

"Remember Alec. We had that NDA done to keep you a mum of certain things. Just wait until everything is in order, and then you can talk to him. The original numbers we discussed, let's go with that....minus 10%, I think I earned that." He smiled again. What a bastard.

The "intern" and the "hamster" stepped in to discuss the mumbo jumbo that they do, and the call was over a few minutes later. Sara x'ed out of the video, and we both just sat on the couch with our hands in our laps.

"Aeron, you see why you needed to see this?"

"Yeah, I do... Can I get you a drink? I need a drink."

"Yes, please, a drink would be fine."

I poured us both a double Makers Mark with a little water and a few ice cubes. I rolled both glasses and handed her one. I took a swig and downed the entire glass. She took a pittance of hers. All I wanted to do was take and finish it. I refrained.

"OK, Sara, Alec was sleeping with this Kyra. What was her last name."

"Bacon."

"Yeah, how did this happen? Do you know the story behind it?"

"I do, and a whole lot more."

It was barely 2:00 pm in the afternoon, and I knew we were in for a long afternoon and night.

Chapter 33

I sat back on the couch and allowed Sara to start and tell the entire story. She found the video on the Comptor Zoom page. It was archived in a special file, and I believe it may have been meant to be deleted. It never was. The video itself was about 14 months old. She downloaded it to her Dropbox account. The video is still on the company Zoom page. She debated on whether to delete it herself but decided against it not being tracked through data analytics. I am not much of an IT guy, but Sara seemed to be. This brought me back to the "intern" and "hamster" who were themselves very IT savvy. The model of a younger woman with high-end computer skills was something that Dan gravitated to. I was still trying to figure out Sara's age and decided to let my curiosity take over.

"Sara, I don't mean to be rude or disrespectful, but can I ask your age?"

"I am 33, and yours?"

"Ha, 50, thank you very much."

She fit the wheelhouse for the age of these women, too. Now, I followed up on the big question.

"How did you get involved with this company, Dan, all of it., I mean, when did you start working for him."

That was the question that opened the floodgates. I was not ready for what I was about to hear. Sara began by going back several years. She grew up in Tallahassee, Florida, a hometown girl going to college at Florida State University. She met her husband, Sam O'Connor, in her sophomore year. They were both computer science majors. Sam grew up in Orlando. The school brought them together. They began dating as normal college kids would. Fell in love and graduated. Sam drew the shortest straw and ended up staying in Tallahassee, where they got jobs, moved in together, and progressed very nicely for early 20s college kids. After nearly 6 years, Sam finally proposed, she accepted. They were married a year later. Her parents helped with the down payment for a little house, and she got pregnant. A complete paint-by-number of the perfect life. Sam Jr. was born in July, and parenthood began. Sara stopped for a moment to compose herself and then continued. She was working on a big project and had to work a marathon week, including a full weekend, to cover a deadline. Sam and Junior wanted to go to Orlando to see his family. She told them to go and was sorry she could not make it. Taking I-10 to I-75, A tropical depression was in full swing. Both being lifelong Florida residents, driving in this type of storm was not a big deal. Sara had little worries. Along the Florida turnpike, about 50 miles from Orlando, things started to turn. The wind gusts of over 70mph came out of nowhere, and the rain was sheets. The Nissan Pathfinder Sam was driving is a great car for these conditions, but before Sam could decide to pull over and wait it out, an older model Ford pickup started to hydroplane in the lane next to him. Before he could react, the truck veered off, slamming his front end. The Pathfinder did a 360 before flipping in the air and being taken by the wind, slamming into the center of the highway overpass. They were both killed instantly. Sara stopped and went to the bathroom.

I picked up the rest of her drink and finished it. Being the shrewd drunk that I am, I went and prepared two more. Sara came back down after roughly 10 minutes. It was obvious she had to get what she needed out so she could continue.

"Sara, you don't have to talk anymore if you don't want to." I handed her the fresh drink.

"I am OK. I want you to know these things so you can help me." She downed the double Makers Mark in one gulp. Impressive.

As she continued, she clarified that it had been about 3 years since her husband and son were killed. The first year was the worst. She had lost everything. Almost her will to live. She was someone who grew up in a deeply Christian religious family. She felt betrayed and blamed God for turning his back on her loyalty to him. She quit her job and moved back home. She fell into a depression that no one in her life could help move on from.

"What changed?" I asked.

"Dan, Dan Rand," she said, wiping more tears away.

After nearly a year of her self-exile from her Church, after being coerced by her parents, she decided to spend Easter Sunday at a service. She did not know what to expect, this is when she first saw and met Dan. The holiday service is always a special thing in her Church. They had a special speaker that day. The head of the Proverbs Church in Georgia was going to do the easter Homily. It was Dan Rand. She was instantly drawn to him. His words and mannerisms spoke to her like nothing since the death of her most beloved. His passion for God, especially women, was something she had never heard in a sermon before. He spoke of the sacred feminine and that "female energy is crucial to the balance of awareness of the collective," and he finished the sermon with "Commit to the work of the LORD, and your plans will be established."

"Hold on a second." I said, "That last line you just said, isn't that the Comptor company vision statement?"

"Yes, and he finishes every sermon with that."

"I had no idea he was that deep into this. He runs his own Church, too?"

"Yeah, he calls it his 'Hobby', it is what he does when not running his company."

She speaks of the first meeting with Dan after the service. She told him about her tragedy. He was the first person to inspire her since it happened. Dan was also drawn to her and asked if they could talk again. She agreed.

"Let me ask, Sara. He seems so wooden and awkward in his company situations; I don't see this guy as being charismatic. What am I missing?"

"Yeah, I know, it is like he is 2 different people. The owner, Dan, is so much different than the spiritual Dan. I had a little work to do to get used to that."

She speeds through the circumstances that got her involved with Dan and the Proverbs church. After a few months and getting to know him and his family, he asks her to come and stay at his compound. She can work for his company. She had the kinds of skills he was looking for.

"Two years later, and here we are. He gave me purpose and appreciated the IT skillset I possessed. The first year was great, I was working intimately with him on the Vivant merger deals and had a lot of meetings with Alec Teacham. The company was growing leaps and bounds."

"So, when did you start to see things change?"

"Well, that is where Ali Howard and Laura Staley come in."

I knew very little about the "intern." The "hamster" was nothing like the girl who worked for me years ago. Sara is starting to fill in some gaps. Ali graduated from Minnesota State University with a computer science degree and attended Harvard for a year before meeting Dan and decided to work with him. She became the number two person in Comptor in less than 3 years.

"So, she is what 24?"

"No, 26."

"My gawd, I was in my 30s when I got to the number two person at Vivant."

"Aeron, it wasn't on merit. She is a bitch, a henchman type. She loves doing dirty work. Her skills are nowhere near where someone in her position should be."

"What about Laura?"

"If you remember, Alec introduced her to Dan, and he was enamored with her right away. I think Dan is fond of her because she isn't very bright. Smart enough to do what he needs her to do, but not someone who isn't going to move up, so to speak."

"Do you like her?"

"No, she is an idiot. I try not to have any conversations with her. It is painful."

I listen to this and feel somewhat vindicated, but I am sure there is more to say about both. I look at the clock. It is almost 7:00 pm. I ask her if she wants to keep talking, and after glancing at the clock herself, she decides it is time to call it a night. We decided to meet the next day. She still has so much more to say.

"Aeron, this gets a lot deeper. I am just scratching the surface. I really do need you to help me. I will explain more tomorrow." She leaves. I take a big breath as I close the door. How am I going to be able to help? I can barely dress these days. I think about dinner and another drink. I abstain from both and just go to bed.

I wake, and I cannot move. I look at my hands, and I am strapped to a table. The room is completely white, with a bright spotlight above me. I start to hear a voice, first faintly, then louder, saying the same phrase over and over. It takes a while to understand the voice. "Conform and Comply," "Conform and Comply," "Conform and Comply," over and over, louder and louder. Wake up, damnit, wake up!! I try to move my hands and feet; I am tied to metal posts on the corners of the table. I close my eyes, and the voice disappears. I open my eyes, and I am surrounded. Everyone is wearing a surgical mask. I see the eyes but cannot decipher who anyone is. I plead, "Who are you! What are you!" each person starts to pull the masks down, the intern, the hamster, Alec, Mom, Dad, Dan, and the last one is right above my head. She pulls her mask down. It is Sara. She touches my forehead and smiles, "Come home with us, commit your work to the LORD, and your plans will be established." "No," I say, "No!" "You have no choice. You are ours now." She brands a cross on my cheek and laughs, "We own you, loser."

Shit!!! Awake and damnit, I pissed my pants again. This has to stop. I cannot take this crap anymore. I get up, grab a pillow, and make my way to the couch, pull my soaked underwear off, and just cry until I fall asleep again.

Chapter 34

I groggily move my way up off the couch. My neck and lower back are killing me. It is sad to think that I was a fined-tune athlete not that many years ago. I did a lot in my past life that I look back on and barely remember, other than the pain of not doing a thing now. I stumble to the kitchen and grab a 5-hour energy to try to get this body started again. I make my way to the couch and realize I am still pantless. Rectify that issue with a pair of David Beckham underwear and Nike sweatpants. I try again to make sense of what has transpired over the last 24 hours. All I can comprehend is that I have brought Sara into these brutal nightmares I am having more and more often. Since she has just given me the tip of the iceberg, I just have to sit back and wait for the rest. I am afraid I am going to disappoint her after she sells all of this to me. I don't have any confidence I can help anyone, even myself. Maybe it is best if I just do not answer the door, tell her to go away, or just figure out something else to let her down. Can I find some other way to get what she wants me to do? To 'need me' is not a very smart option.

There was a knock on the door around 8:45 am. I stayed seated and let the door knock again, a little harder. The third time, I heard, "I know you are up, Aeron. Open the door, please." I can't let that one go and open for her. She rushes in. I do a double take out-side my front door again, looking for neighbors. The lo-cals tend to talk around these parts.

"Hi, Good Morning." She throws her computer bag on the coffee table and starts to unpack again.

"Want some coffee, 5-hour energy, a valium?" She stops in her tracks.

"You have valium?"

"No, I don't, just a joke."

"Funny, Ha, coffee is fine." She is deadly serious as she prepares to ramp up the discussion from the previous day.

"Look, Sara, I have been thinking all night. I don't know if I want to get involved. My life is pretty damn shitty, and I am starting to like it..."

She interrupts me, "No it's not, stop it. I don't need this pathetic bullshit from you. I know what happened to you. I know your story. I had a conversation with Alec about you. I know about your ex-wife and the fucked-up childhood. He told me a lot about you. You really made an impact on him."

"Really, he said that?"

"Yes, for the record, he is still a shit who fucked you over and his family, but he genuinely has or had a soft spot for you. He told me a lot of things during our downtime with the negotiating process."

"I don't know what to say about all that."

"Well, I will say that whatever pity party you are doing, you better snap out of it because we got work to do."

"Can I at least get some more information first?"

"Yes, sit down, this may take a while."

Sara begins again and starts to weave the rest of her interactions with Dan, the Church, and the team. Part of working at the compound is that you have to commit to the Church, but not necessarily in a religious way. It is a bit sly, but it is more of a pledge of loyalty to the company. Dan is adept at balancing his company with his Church. Sara seems to think that to motivate his employees he uses his 'Temple'. This is a building on his compound where his employees meet for motivational speeches, team-building events, and overall positive vibes about work and spirituality. She then goes into a darker direction about an interaction with Dan on a business trip back to Tallahassee. Sara had not seen her parents in almost 6 months and wanted to catch up with them. Dan coincidentally had a meeting with a potential business partner at the same time. Instead of staying with her parents, Dan insisted that she stay in his hotel to work on prep and give them time to connect on a deeper divine level.

"Let me have a minute to gather myself." Sara lets her vulnerability creep in a bit as she takes a break from the story.

"Can I get you anything, a drink or something?"

"No, and that's another thing. No more drinking while we are going through this. We don't have a lot of time, and I need you clear and 100%."

"What do you need me to do, Sara?"

"Just be patient. I will get there."

She refocuses and starts again. She was staying in the same hotel as Dan, and he asked her to dinner. She thought it was with the client, but it was just the two of them. This is when Dan started to dig into his philosophy. He started to explain his take on the sacred feminine and why it has been so important to the growth of his business. He explained the "Moon Goddess" and how the stages of a woman are the Maiden-birth, Mother-life, and Crone-death. He learned about this during a downturn in his business about a decade earlier as he was trying to regroup and get back on his feet. Over time he came to an epiphany that the retrieval of feminine energy was his key to being successful and is essential for women to have control over men. He believed that men had betrayed him in all aspects of his life, especially in his business dealings. So, to get back what he felt was due to him is to use the power of the sacred feminine to attack the weakness in all males to bring them down. He determined this to be sexual ecstasy and bodily satisfaction. This is what motivated him to start his Church to coincide with the rebranding of his business. It was a lot for her to take in. Her head was spinning with all of it. They made their way back to the hotel; he asked her into his room to finish the conversation. She reluctantly agreed; he poured her another drink, and that was the last she remembered from the night. She woke up next to him in the morning, half-clothed with a headache. She gathered her things and went back to her room.

"I took the longest shower of my life that morning. I did not know what happened, but I knew what happened." Tears rolled down her face.

"He raped you?"

"I don't know, I think so, but we never talked about it."

"You didn't say anything to him?"

"No, the next time I saw him, we got right back into the business dealings."

She continued with more of the trip. They were joined by another member of the company, Katie Horton. She was another young IT specialist who was brought in to discuss with a potential client his computer portals and capabilities. Sara was instructed to just take notes. They spent the afternoon with Bill Wright, president of Killen Enterprises. The meeting then went into dinner with the four of them. The interactions with Bill and Katie were going beyond just informational. Outward flirting with Dan sitting like a maestro, smiling and encouraging. Innuendo ensued; Bill invited everyone to the bar for more drinks. She looked at Dan who just stood up and told the two of them to go ahead. Dan wanted me to go back to his room with him to break down minutes from the day's meeting events. Katie and Bill made their way to the bar, and Sara and Dan left. On the way back to the room, Dan stated to Sara, "That is the power of the sacred feminine. Remember that."

"So, Katie seduced Bill?"

"Absolutely."

"Did you know what was going on at that point?"

"No, not fully, but the female intuition was kicking in."

"What happened after that?"

"3 weeks later, Bill sold Killen to Comptor at a lower price that was first negotiated."

"Was there a video of that, too?"

"No, I am certain that the confrontation was in person."

"My god, so Dan sets up these business owners with women from the company, they sleep with them, get pics or something else, and then blackmails them in selling their companies?"

"Yes, and it is genius in a way. He only negotiates with companies that are ready to sell or on the fence about it. Bill Wright reminded me so much of Alec. We had been discussing a merger with him for almost a year. Dan just chose his best way to close the deal."

"The sacred feminine bribery approach."

"You can call it that."

"Sara, what did you do after this?"

"I needed to figure out who was working for this company and this church."

"You mean Cult, Sara."

"I don't know if it is a Cult."

"Oh my god, yes, it is a Cult."

"Do you know anything about Cults, Aeron?"

"Not really, except maybe Jim Jones or David Koresh stuff."

"Well, maybe we need to find out more about that."

"Sara, I need to know more about this church and the people in it."

"Aeron, it is just women and whatever children they have."

"Really, can you explain more about that?"

Sara explains how Dan and his team described the Church to her when she joined after being hired by the company. It is a prerequisite to working at Comptor. It is framed as more of a spiritual organization. He calls it the Proverbs Church to get a tax break from the government. What happens is more about female empowerment and exposing men to get the most out of life and business. All the women who work for Comptor are either single, divorced, or, like Sara, widowed. Nearly half the female employees are widowed. Dan believes he is an innovator who will take the business world to a new level by building his business empire and feeding his profits into Proverbs to trust and empower women to strengthen his relationship with God. Ali Howard is his right-hand person with not only business but the Church. She left her husband before Dan promoted her to Chief of Staff. Laura Staley told her that. Sara realized early on that if any gaps needed to be filled, the "hamster" couldn't keep a secret to save her life.

"So, Ali is a part of all this. What about Laura?"

"Dan didn't promote her until after she divorced her husband."

"She is a part too."

"Everyone is. There is no choice."

"Even the men in the company?"

"I am sorry. Let me rephrase. No men. Only the females in the company. Dan is the only man."

"How do you feel about this female empowerment angle he takes with this?"

"It is bullshit, Aeron. He doesn't want to 'empower' us for our talents. He wants to use our sexuality to get what he wants. He wants his business empire, and that is all that matters."

"What I am gathering is that with his past and insecurity around men, he created this female, whatever the fuck it is, to be able to be the businessman he wants to be."

"That about covers it."

"So, all these women are loyal to Dan and Proverbs."

"Fiercely."

"Would you be OK if I get some more information about Cults?"

"Sure, I need to leave now, anyway. I am talking to a reporter today that I connected with from FSU."

"Reporter?"

"Yes, Joanie Woodward, Washington Post. We had the same major first couple years and she changed over to journalism."

"What is the plan, Sara?"

"I will tell you after I talk to her."

Sara gathers her evidence and leaves. We again make plans to meet the next day. I will keep my word and not drink, but I need to keep busy and not wallow. I have work to do. I need to find out more about Cults beyond just a documentary.

Chapter 35

I sit at my computer to figure out what direction I need to go with my research. A Google search is not the best approach. I have no idea about Cults. I don't have any connections. I contemplate Cults as some sort of mental issue for people. I decided to reach out to the only person I know who may point me in the right direction. I emailed Roseanne Rosario. I waited a few hours to get a response. She is curious about why I reached out to her. We scheduled a video call. She was surprised to hear from me so soon.

"Hi Aeron!" She looked pleased to see me.

"Hi Roseanne, good to see you."

"You look well, have you figured your insurance situation out and want to start back up with the coaching?"

"No, I haven't gotten around to that yet, I am not calling you about me. I have a situation I am dealing with and wondering if you can point me in the right direction."

"OK, I will see if I can help."

"Do you anything about cults?"

She paused for a moment; a bit blindsided by the question. "Yes...Yes, I do."

"I mean, do you know a lot about Cults? I need a ton of information."

"Aeron. Are you getting involved with something? With your mental state, you are prime for grooming."

"No, No, No, Roseanne, this is not about me... Well, it is sort of about me, I just need information."

"OK, I know a lot about this stuff, a whole hell of a lot. A cult deeply affected my life and family."

"Really, in what way?"

She paused again to compose herself. "I can't get into it much now, but my sister was involved in a cult while I was in college, and she ended up...taking her own life. Pushed me into the direction of mental health. I tried to save her and failed, the system failed too. It really betrayed my family. She betrayed all of us by not being stronger. Look can we talk in a few hours? I have some appointments to get through."

"Yes, please, let's talk after dinner time tonight."

I texted Sara and let her know I may be able to get some quality information to share when we meet. She responds that she had a great meeting with Joanie Woodward. We can start talking about "The Plan" when we meet next. I have no idea what this plan is, but I have been learning a little about Sara over the last few days. She is quite a determined person.

I have dinner. Continue the struggle from having a cocktail. I start pacing my living room waiting to hear from Roseanne. She calls and asks if would I rather talk on the phone or video. I chose video. I wanted to see her face as we were talking. It is after 6:00 pm and we get on the call. Roseanne looks much different than in our coaching sessions. Her hair is down, wearing a grey T-Shirt, sitting in what looks like a home office. She looks down at her desk, gazes up, and asks.

"Are you ready for this?"

I pause for a moment, seeing the pain in her face, "Yes, Roseanne. I am ready."

To give me context Roseanne begins to discuss her sister, Kiki. Six years younger than her, sweet, impressionable, gullible. When Kiki was 15, she met a boy a few years older than her. She fell head over heels for him. This boy and his family were involved in a Church organization called "Hexagone." The leader of this Church was called 'The Mystic.' From what she found out, they had an affiliation with Jehovah's Witnesses but broke off. The 'Mystic' began his own church. Teenage boys were groomed to recruit for the organization, to help build and populate the congregation. Kiki's boyfriend was instructed to find 'his girl'. Roseanne's sister was the prize to bring back. It did not take long for Kiki to become indoctrinated. They used "Love Bombing" techniques. Kiki was accepted and loved by everyone unconditionally. The Mystic took a shine to her and brought her into the inner circle. Over a short period, Kiki was manipulated to be totally controlled. She was instructed to bear a child. She became pregnant within a month of being with her boyfriend. She began to stop coming home and the family started to get the authorities involved. Roseanne ended up leaving school to come home and try to help her parents save Kiki.

The Mystic was arrested and then let go. Kiki could not be located, and no evidence of wrongdoing was found. The Police just looked at Kiki as a runaway who went on an escapade with her boyfriend. Meanwhile, Kiki was being moved from house to house from other members of the church. Different elders called 'Enforcers' continued to lie and use Kiki's naivete against her.

After 3 months Roseanne finally received a call from Kiki. She was in distress, struggling with medical issues during the pregnancy, With the belief system she would not go to a traditional hospital. Like Jehovah Witnesses, the Hexagone did not believe in customary medical care. She was directed to pray for the baby and to heal herself. Roseanne begged her to leave, but Kiki was fully indoctrinated. She wanted Roseanne to go back to the family and begin to pray for her. The more that people who loved Kiki prayed, the quicker she would heal. Roseanne begged to see her, Kiki refused. She kept saying "Just pray for me, please." After six months of searching, Roseanne met up with a former member of Hexagone member who had met Kiki a few months back. The true horror of the church was to come out. The Mystic ruled the clan with an iron fist. The young girls were held and forced to have baby after baby. They performed mind control exercises to break each girl down to a point where all that mattered was having children for the church. Some had serious health issues. Proper medical care was not provided to anyone. They would do ritual praying above the sick girl and drive the 'illness spirit' out of them. Roseanne was talking so fast. So much to say, I could hardly keep up.

"What happened to Kiki, Roseanne?"

She sat staring at me through the screen, grabbed a towel and wiped her face, looked back down at her desk before replying, "She died...She killed herself. A few members were so disturbed that they called the police after finding Kiki hanging in her bedroom closet. My beautiful sister had a miscarriage at 5 ½ months. She was guilted and punished so badly for not saving her baby that she could not take the shame."

I just stared back at her speechless.

"The police, detectives, did nothing. The Cult got away with it. They could not even prove that the boyfriend impregnated her. There were no remnants of the baby. My Kiki...This is why I changed majors and became a psychotherapist. The mental health coaching helps pay the bills."

"Oh god, Roseanne, I was not expecting...."

"No one does, I never talk about it. Why do you need information on cults, Aeron?"

"I believe the company that fired me, the owner runs a cult under the rouse of a business. I met a woman a few days ago who gave me proof that my former mentor and boss was blackmailed into selling his company. I never had to deal with anything like this before."

"OK, I am going to give you the rundown on cults and what to do and look for, I think that will help you identify if this is the same thing. If what you are dealing with is a Cult, you must stop it, by whatever means necessary. Understand that anyone involved is in extreme danger."

"I understand." I take a deep breath and Roseanne pulls out a notebook and begins to explain to me what I am looking for.

"You better take notes, Aeron." I flip my legal pad to a clean sheet. I don't think I will be using just one page.

Roseanne goes into her spiel about cults. I have a feeling she has done this exercise before. The passion she shows in her description has an air of longing for her sister. Her telling people about the dangers of cults is a way to keep Kiki's legacy alive. She shows no emotion in her explanation, it is all business.

She starts with how cults draw people in. The "Love Bombing" aspect. The person is loved immediately, taken into a cradle of protection by the group. The Leader is then brought in to explain the purpose of love and togetherness. The person was "chosen" to be a part of the special organization. The cycle continues to create dependency, strip boundaries and convinces the person that the way of the cult is the only way. The leader presents him or herself as a prophet. They often twist meanings of actual religious scripture. Unfortunately, sexuality in some way is often used.

"What Hexagone did to Kiki was use her own natural personality and instincts against her. Her fear and guilt mechanisms were exploited by either the leader or his 'enforcers'. These are chosen people by the leader to make sure all follow the simple adage to 'conform and comply.'"

"So how does the cult brainwash a person? I would think that people would recognize these things and get out."

"Aeron, that is not as easy as you would think. This is where the mental health aspect of this comes in."

She goes into what is called 'Character Assassination'. The 'Enforcers' or leader recognize if a member is getting out of line or questioning the purpose. That is when the mind games start. The person is made to feel worthless by breaking down emotionally, exposing personal fears or weakness. The members attack the person in question who blames them for the issues they are feeling. Questioning loyalty, and then using peer pressure to break them. Once the person submits, the 'Love Bombing' starts again.

"I figured they used all these actions on Kiki. When I spoke to members of Hexagone that defected they told me about severe mind control, information control and time control. This is a classic cult trait. Control you, control messaging and keep you busy, often sleep deprived to keep the person from thinking clearly."

"So, what happens when you want to escape?"

"Most of the time you are so brainwashed that you need to be physically removed. This is where relationship control comes in. You are restricted from seeing friends and family who are not a part of the cult. We as a family knew we had to find Kiki and remove her on our own. This is where the issues arise with the authorities. They either didn't have the time or didn't care to help us. By the time we were able to figure out where she may have been, it was too late."

Roseanne talks about some of the other trick's cults use to coerce members into staying. Telling lies about family, friends, or the outside world. Everyone is the enemy except the "family" or inner circle of the cult.

"The scary part is that most of the 'Leaders' of these cults are mentally ill or sociopathic. This has an even greater effect on the members of the group. The psychological damage they have done keeps the member in place and trying to deprogram is so difficult. This is why suicide rates among people in cults is so high, whether they stay in or get out."

"What is the goal of these cult leaders, Roseanne?"

"Gold, Glory and Girls...more succinctly, money, power and sex."

"Oh my God, I am dealing with a cult Roseanne. The aspirations of this guy, Dan is all those things."

"Then you have to do something about it. With whoever this woman is, but remember, you are more than likely going to be on your own. Unless you have concrete and substantial information on improprieties, no one is going to help you. You may be the one they will go after for harassment."

"I got it. You have no idea how much this means to me, Roseanne."

She smiles before responding "This could be your way to make everything right, Aeron. Therapy comes in all shapes and sizes. A little revenge wouldn't be a bad thing."

"Maybe I will find some purpose after all."

"Maybe, just don't tell anyone you got the information from me. I don't know how ethical what I just discussed with you is." she chuckles.

"Secret safe with me, Roseanne. I hope you know, Kiki is still with us because of you. You are going to save a lot of lives because of what you know. I hope I can do the same."

"Just go to work, clock is ticking."

"I will."

We ended the video call and I instantly reached out to Sara to let her know we needed to get together as early as possible in the morning. She responds that she will as soon as she finishes with Joanie in the morning. I almost asked her to come by immediately, but after 3 hours on a call with Roseanne, my mind was fully exhausted.

Chapter 36

I had my best night of sleep in months. No dreams, nearly eight full hours, new energy with the information I was still processing from Roseanne. Sara texted me around 9:15 a.m. that she was on her way. I received the knock on the door and answered with a smile on my face that she had seen before.

"You look chipper this morning."

"Well, Sara, I had a great day yesterday gathering what I think we need to know for what we are dealing with."

"Look at you." She gave a coy look in response.

"Short and sweet; Comptor, Proverbs, and Dan are all a cult."

"OK, tell me more."

"Have a seat."

I spent the next hour briefing her on everything Roseanne told me from the previous night, including the tragedy of her sister, Kiki. I had to slow down at times. I was so focused and boosted by what was going on. I was in a place where I felt so much strength that Sara had to stop me a few times to get her own bearings. This mindset felt good.

"So, we are dealing with a cult. Not all the factors fit, but enough of them do to know that we are in an urgent situation here. After speaking with Joanie, we got some things in motion."

"Yes, Joanie, what is she doing? And what is the plan, anyway? All I know now is we have to do something."

"We are. She is on her way to Berlin, and so are we."

"Berlin, Georgia? We are going to the compound."

"Yeah, we have to find more proof. What I shared with Joanie was a good start but nothing that the Post would want to cover as is. Plus, if we want to get the authorities involved, we need a lot more."

Sara pulls out ten files from her bag and throws them on the table.

"This is your job. These are ten companies that Comptor has acquired that I know of. I got these from the main office on the compound. You need to get your work done quickly; I need to have these back in the cabinets when I go back on Monday."

"What do you want me to do with these?"

"Alec told me you are a wiz at company research. When you two were building Vivant, he had you do all the recon of the companies you were engaging. Whatever you do, I need you to find out everything you can about these companies and contracts. The information we need has to be in there."

"OK, so what do we do now?"

"Pack a bag. We are flying out to Tallahassee and driving to Berlin. Joanie is going to meet us at a hotel tomorrow afternoon."

I pack light, get on Expedia to purchase two plane tickets to Tallahassee and a rental car. I was able to get us out on a red eye, with no layovers and landing around 5:00 a.m. I start to peruse through the files and get my mind rolling on what I used to be good at. Time to dust those skills off. We head out to the airport; Sara is going to park her car in the hope of coming back next weekend to pick it up and drive back home. She does not seem concerned about the vehicle. She is completely focused on the time crunch we are under. We will be arriving in Tallahassee early Saturday morning. We need to get as much information as possible before she returns from her "vacation" on Monday morning.

"Aeron, we have to get all this work done this weekend. Ali is relocating to Berlin starting on Monday. She sold her house in Minnesota and is moving into the compound. Dan wants her close by so they can ramp up additional acquisitions they are working on. Ali isn't going to want me around. I already know they plan on moving me back to virtual and off the compound."

"Why would they do that?"

"I think I am not progressing with the instruction at the speed they want. So, removing me from the compound and back home is what they do with certain females who have a use to them, but not at the level they want."

"Can I ask why that is, Sara? With what I have learned about cults recently, you don't seem to be getting caught up with this like most people do."

"Well, I guess I am a little smarter than they give me credit for. Plus, Dan betrayed my trust and, more than likely, my body. I want to take that son of a bitch down. He took advantage of my pain and grieving. He told me that my husband and son dying was meant to happen because God wanted her to be with him. Fuck him." She throws her notebook across my dining room.

"Looks like we both have scores to settle here, Sara."

"Let's head to the airport. Grab your computer, Aeron. I am sure you will need that, too."

We leave, get checked in, and are on the plane with no issues. Easy takeoff, 30,000 feet connect into Wi-Fi, I start getting to work. Going through the company files first. Want to try and get a feel for each company and the contracts. Nothing crazy. Everything seems consistent. Standard boilerplate stuff. Each contract starts with a heavy down payment to the company, and the remaining money is paid off within 18 months. Each former president continues some sort of role through the merger. Like Alec did for Vivant. Every merger had the same thing in common, the original company name was eliminated after six months. Like they never existed. The Vivant file is in there, as well. It is hard to go through that one. So much comes back to me, and I try to just focus on connecting the dots. I see the NDA and still cannot believe Alec allowed himself to get caught up in that. I decided to start the online process to check some additional financial information. I am beginning to understand the patterns, and I am curious about whether what happened with Vivant was happening across the board.

I used an online platform to research companies and get access to public records. I stumbled on this about seven years ago when we were starting to expand, and it was incredibly helpful. Before I could dig into this, our plane landed. That was the fastest flight I can remember.

Sara was exhausted and slept through the whole flight. I nudged her.

"Wake up, sleepyhead, landed."

"How is the research going?"

"I got pretty much all I could out of the files. I need to go online and connect some things. I am seeing some patterns that should be easy to follow up on."

"Let's get going. We can be in Berlin in about 90 minutes, and we have a room at a Holiday Inn right outside of town. Joanie is meeting us there at 4:00 p.m."

The 90-minute drive takes more like 70. Saturday morning and Sara's familiarity with these smaller state roads in southern Georgia felt like autopilot for her. We arrived at the motel around 7:30 a.m. We checked in, and I settled into my work. Sara goes out to get coffee, breakfast, and a newspaper. It had not even hit me yet that I was going on 24 hours without sleep. The adrenaline had taken over, and after a large 24-ounce Dunkin' coffee and two glazed donuts, I was knee-deep in my research. Sara lay back down and read the newspaper. She knew not to converse with me. I am serving a purpose now for this mission. I was doing what she needed me to do.

I started with company #1, then moved to company #2, then #3, and #4. But after about 6 1/2 hours, I was beginning to fade. Sara had dosed off, and I went ahead and rested my eyes. That did not last long, and I was wrestled out of my mini-slumber.

"Wake up, we are still working. You can sleep after the meeting with Joanie."

"Sorry, I guess an old man like me doesn't have the same staying power anymore."

"Just keep going, it's important."

I was again determined. Sara seemed to have a way of motivating me since the 'pity party' reference back at my house. It felt good to have a purpose. I went through the remaining companies. Took about ten pages of notes on my legal pad. It was almost 4:00 p.m., and I was about ready to brief her on my findings.

Sara and I sit at a round table in the room, like the first meeting at the library. This time, we are not face-to-face. We sit side by side. I have my notes, and the computer screen prompts me to the site I use for my research. I am confident. This is definitely my wheelhouse when I begin to talk.

"There are a few things I noticed right away. Seven of the ten companies, including Vivant, were not mergers. They were acquisitions, which is a little different than what Dan and Alec told all of us when this went down. This is why Alec and the six other companies kept the president on with a figurehead title. Mergers change the leadership structure completely."

"So what, why is that important?"

"Because they convinced us, and probably the other companies did as well, that this was a merger, and everything is going to be all kumbaya. Then, after six months, the original company name is completely removed. I didn't understand that at first, but give me a few, and I will tie it together."

I then start to break down the similarities of all the deals. The seven companies I found all had male CEO's. One had a gay male CEO and the other 2 were female CEO's. The difference between the seven and the three was the seven all sold their company for significantly less than the fair market value at the time. Sometimes up to 20% less. The other three were sold exactly at the fair market value rate. I was then curious and investigated when Dan's first company went under. He started Comptor ten years earlier. His first company, Sustence, filed for bankruptcy a year earlier than that. The year he filed it, we had our most profitable year to date and had acquired four accounts that were directly attached to Sustence. I am sure that chapped Dan pretty well.

"Aeron, he wanted revenge for tanking his first company."

"Yeah, I am starting to think that too. Stay with me here."

I then explained how I probed what Dan was doing with all the assets from the seven companies he obtained. After he eliminated any remnants of the former companies, he was selling the assets from all those companies to the highest bidders, and I traced those funds to an account, Proverbs Access LLC. The other three companies without the male heterosexual CEOs, he kept in place. I figured this is what he is using to fund his church.

"So, this is what he is going to do to Vivant next."

"That is what I figure. Nothing has happened yet, but I am sure it is coming."

"That is great work, Aeron. Now I see why Alec kept you around."

I smiled, "I am not completely worthless."

She walked up and kissed me on the cheek, "You are alright when not feeling sorry for yourself. You smell, go take a shower. Joanie will be here in a few minutes. We have more to go over."

I get into the shower and wash off everything from the last 30 hours or so. I let the water wash over me and think that I am still capable. I am certainly not in control here. This is Sara's show, and I am OK with being a cog in her motivational process. Sara raps on the door.

"Joanie is here. Let's go. This is no marathon session. What are you, a woman?"

I laugh. "Be right there."

I got out, dried off, and put on clean underwear, the same jeans I had been wearing, and a Colorado flag T-shirt. It was what I still call home, sort of. I came to an unusual conclusion that a pair of clean underwear can buy a person a couple of hours when seriously sleep-deprived.

I reentered the room. Sara and Joanie were now occupying the table. No room for three, I sat on the end of the bed, prepared to be a spectator for this next session.

"Aeron, this is Joanie Woodward. I told you that we went to FSU together, and she is going to help us."

Joanie looked like a true go-getter. Even sitting, she looked tall, I would say around 5'8", with long black hair, no curls or frills. Hazel eyes. Eyes that could see through a liar. V-neck T-shirt and a look you would expect from a reporter.

"Hi Aeron, Sara has told me a little about you. This could be an incredible story if everything comes together."

Sara and I bring Joanie up to speed on all the information we have come up with on our end. Sara brings up a video that she wants both of us to see before we move on to Joanie's discoveries. She wants both of us to see Dan in action during one of his "Reflections" assemblies. These would be called sermons in any other church setting, but Dan, always the innovator, wanted to decipher his with the branding he felt fit. She only wanted us to watch a few minutes and didn't want to waste our time with all his "Bullshit." What I witnessed shocked me. Not that what Dan said was all profound. He was just different in this setting. The awkward, weird, deferring business leader was replaced by what looked like Oral Roberts in his prime. My mother loved watching OR on Sunday mornings when I grew up. He was this demonstrative, charismatic man who held his audience in the palm of his hands. I never got it. He just seemed like some weird old guy to me. My dad just rolled his eyes when getting coffee on Sunday, burying himself in a newspaper until it was over. Dan Rand on a pulpit was not the man I saw while with Comptor. He appeared as if he was born to be on that stage. His body language, mannerisms and delivery were poetic. Perfect for the moment. I realized that this was where he wanted to be. The crowd was full of about 300 women, no male in sight. This was his utopia. Sara turned it off after nine minutes.

"Just wanted to give you both some flavor of what we are dealing with." She was all business.

"I cannot believe this is the guy I dealt with. Honestly, I didn't think he had this in him."

"Dan is full of surprises."

"Maybe a few more." Joanie chimed in.

Sara and I just glanced at each other. It was time for Joanie to get started.

Joanie begins briefing us on the information she had acquired over the last 24 hours.

"When I arrived, I started looking at what goes on in this town, especially any criminal-type happenings. This place is as squeaky clean as you can find."

"What do you mean?" I asked.

"There is literally no crime in this town at all, and if there is, someone is covering it up, pretty good. Not one homicide, missing person, robbery, rape. It is friggin' strange. Also, check this out, every store or place of business I visited yesterday, all women."

Sara spoke, "Yeah, I think Dan really influences the businesses in the city to hire women. He is the head of the City Council, which is all women, except for him."

"Sara, have any employees who were a part of the compound left in the last year?"

"Yes, about six months ago, I remember, two left abruptly, and we did not get any information on what happened to them. Sophie Novak and Kim Fried. I can pull up their HR information."

Sara pulled up the contact information for Joanie.

"I have a hunch about this. Let's get back together on Monday afternoon. There is something really weird going on around here."

Joanie took the information she needed and left.

"Sara, if these two employees tried to leave on their own, who knows what could have happened to them."

"We don't have much of an off boarding process. We have not lost any employees who are a part of the compound since I got here. That is what is strange about Sophie and Kim."

"What did Dan say about them?"

"Nothing, he honestly didn't say anything. He just moved on."

I was on my last legs for the day and sat back on the bed.

"I am just going to bed; this has felt like a marathon today."

"I know, Aeron. Thank you for the information. It is going to help tie some things up."

"Do you want me to call down to the office and get a rollaway bed brought up here?" The room rented had just one queen-sized bed. "Or I can just sleep on the floor."

"Don't be silly. We can just lay together. I think we are both so tired that it won't matter anyway."

"OK, I am not going to bother even changing." I just roll over, grab a pillow, and pass out within a couple of minutes.

A few hours later, I awoke and saw that Sara was still on her computer at the table. She looks as focused and intent as if the day just started. I smile and turn back over. I am asleep again in almost no time.

I wake up in the room and look back over at Sara. She is still, as if frozen. "Sara...Sara..." no answer. I get up out of bed and begin to walk to her. There is a rap on the door. I turn and walk over, "Who is it?" no answer. I open and look to the right and left. Nothing. I step out into the hallway; the door closes behind me. I reach for the doorknob, and it disintegrates in my hand. The mist rises in the hallway. I know I have been in this dream before and keep telling myself, "Wake Up!! Wake Up!!!" I slowly start walking down the hallway, and the mist thickens. The voices start again. Male, female, female, male. I turn and make my way back to my door. The knob is back. I turned it, and the door opened. I walked back into the room. Sara turns her head up to me and smiles. "Sara, are you OK?" She just stares first at me and then behind me. She says, "Turn around." I look over my right shoulder and then turn completely around. Nothing. I look back at Sara, and she is gone. I turn around again. It is the "intern," she grabs me by the throat, smiles, and her teeth fall to the floor. "We have her now. You can't do anything, loser." My arms cannot move, and I begin to black out. The "intern" finishes, "You are nothing. We have her, and we own you..."

I wake up, breathing heavily. I immediately check my pants, still dry. Sara is now lying in bed, her back to me and I can hear her breathing. True sleep breathing, not snoring, just restful. I turn again, and we are now back-to-back. I have not shared a bed with a woman in over three years. It felt good to feel the presence and hear her breath. I fell asleep one last time, and I think I will feel safe, at least until the morning.

Chapter 37

I feel the sun on my back through a crack in the curtain and know that it is morning. I roll over on my back to look at Sara. She is still sleeping; she has no idea how much I am just enjoying watching her. I close my eyes and think of Tara in the mornings when we woke up together. I never felt like I would have a bad day when I awakened next to her. I would touch her shoulder or hip, or just spoon her those last few minutes before we made the decision on how the day was going to start. I just loved to smell her in the morning. It has been so long that I have forgotten that smell, and as with everything, it is a sad, lost chapter in my life that will never return. I looked back at Sara and wished I could smell her just to rekindle something, again. I snap out of it just in time for her to rise out of her slumber. She turns over.

"Morning." I smile.

"Morning, what time is it?" she smiles back.

I pull my phone off the side table, "7:43."

"Wow, I guess we needed that sleep."

"So, Sara, what is the plan, today?"

"I...We need to go to the compound today."

"K, why?"

"Well #1, I need to get these files back to where they belong, and you are going to look in on the Sunday "Ritual" meeting."

"Ritual meeting?"

"Yes, this is where Dan gathers all his leaders, and they go through these female empowerment exercises. I am going to be a part of this today."

"You?"

"Yeah, I am one of Dan's leaders. I have to do this, so nothing looks strange to him. I set up a hidden camera and mic before I left to meet you. You need to be within five hundred feet of the building to be able to watch this. I have a location in the woods behind the building where you can look and hear what is going on."

"How are we going to get on the property?"

She smiles, "I have my ways, don't you worry."

We both shower and dress, grab coffee, and head out to the compound. We pass the front entrance. There is a twelve -foot-high wrought iron fence that looks as if it completely encircles the property. The gate is a Hambledon wrought, dual swing open, with lettering on the left "Pro" and the right "Verbs." We drive until the fencing ends and shortly after coming across a dirt road that guides along the side of the fencing. Sara drives the dirt road until it ends about a half mile up.

"End of the line. You walk from here." She puts the car in park.

"Couldn't have picked a better day." I sarcastically stated. The sunshine that started our day was long gone and a storm had rolled in, and a steady rain was falling. "Where am I walking to?"

"See those trees, follow the little path next to them. You will see a small white line on each tree to the right, follow the white lines until you run into this tiny little building. It looks like an abandoned outhouse, but it's not. I used some old woodworking skills my dad taught me and built that a while back. When you go in, unlock the box and you will have everything you need to see and listen into everything." She hands me the key to the box. "The Ritual starts exactly at noon, so don't get sidetracked. Part of why I need you in that room is to make sure everything is recording properly and that the Wi-Fi adapter I set up doesn't kick out. Without that, we lose connection."

"Got it, boss." I saluted her and she rolled her eyes.

"Now go, I am heading to the back staff entrance and going to get these files placed back in the filing cabinets." The urgency in her voice was evident.

She hands me a rain parka she had in the backseat, and I begin my journey to the "faux" outhouse. It didn't take very long for me to get to the location. I was impressed with her craftsmanship on this. It really looked like an old-school "shitbox" you would see in a John Wayne western. I stepped in. The box was on the floor and a folding chair was leaning up against the side wall of the building. I unfolded and sat down. Unlocked the box. Inside was an iPad and a Wi-Fi adapter with a note that said, "Turn me on." My mind raced a little when I read that. I turned the adapter on. Wi-Fi coverage was good. Booted up the iPad. She had a portable battery pack in the box as well, just in case the batteries ran low. Another set of instructions walked me through how to pull up the video and the sound. All I needed to remember was to push the "record" setting on the app that was being used for this. I am sure I wouldn't screw that up. I looked at my phone, "11:53 am." A few minutes to spare. I stepped out to take a pee and get my mind ready for what I was about to see.

The meeting began precisely at noon. Sara did a great job of placing the camera. I was able to count fifteen women in the room. At Dan's side was Ali Howard, the "Intern." Everyone in the room was wearing black slacks and a white T-shirt with an emblem that I had a hard time deciphering at first but after dialing in for a minute, it resembled two crescent moons with the shape of a female in the center. It looks almost designed like a traditional religious symbol with the female representing Jesus on the cross. Below the symbol were the words 'PROVERBS' and in small letters below that 'sacred feminine'. Dan began the meeting.

"Welcome Leaders. The world is but a creation, woman is the creator. Feminine is the idol and with you, all the power!"

All the women repeated in unison "We have the power!"

"And our Motto, 'SACRED FEMININE!'"

They all repeated.

"Commit your work to the Lord, and your plans will be established."

Dan sat in his chair behind him. It was not a traditional chair, it looked like a mini throne. The 'intern' then took over the summit. It was more of a traditional work meeting with her. She went through the minutes from the last meeting. Gave "shout-outs" to leaders who were doing exceptional things within the company and announced her relocation to the compound as Comptor was looking to go to the next level.

Several more acquisitions were in the works. She proceeded to take nearly twenty minutes to go through all six of them. Most were in the Northeast corridor, but there was one in the Jacksonville area. It was revealed that Sara's transfer from the compound was to focus on that contract with another member of the group and Dan. Sara was moving back home; the upcoming week would be her last on the property. I knew then we were under the gun for many reasons. The group then participated in a team-building event, that was half religious-trivia and half office-Olympics style. There were three teams of five women each. Sara stood more distant than the rest of the women, who were eager to be front and center to win this contest. The trivia was Quizzo style with the intern reading off questions and the teams filling out a sheet collectively. After the questions were answered and graded, they proceeded to the office-Olympic portion of the event. Five events, one for each team member. "Rubberband archery," "pencil javelin," "ball trash can toss," "paperclip necklace," and "ring toss." All these were so familiar because me and Alec would do these events at Vivant's year-end holiday party or mid-summer barbeque. Had a feeling the "hamster" may have stolen these from us. This all took another thirty minutes or so. Dan was cheerleading, giving high-fives to all the ladies. He was in his element. After the winners were announced, the room became more subdued again. Dan again took the pulpit.

"Sacred women, I am so proud of all of you. You show great strength and ingenuity. Remember these traits each day as we continue to grow, to do things differently than any other company. We bring the power of all of you with the lord to create something beautiful and masterful!"

He then finishes by peeling off more scripture.

"Proverbs 14:23 – All hard work brings a profit, but mere talk leads only to poverty...Proverbs 18:9 —

One who is slack in her work is sister to one who destroys." He added "sister" instead of "brother" to that one, I still recall a little from Sunday school.

He finishes with one last rant.

"With all that I have studied and prayed for; women always have cradled the mysteries of life, death, and rebirth within the cocoon of the female flesh. You have the power of healing, balancing, and taking the power you possess of our mother in the earth. We hold these mysteries sacred within us, as I, as your Shephard, will carry you like babies in the womb. Now, go out and do the will of the feminine and make Comptor the best within your spirit."

Everyone in the room hugs, a few are crying, and more seem completely energized by what has transpired over the last hour and fifteen minutes. Dan was in complete control, again. I was stunned that this was the same man who months earlier was tripping all over himself during Zoom meetings that I attended.

I make sure everything is recorded properly and turn off the iPad and Wi-Fi adapter. I did not know what to do from here. I guess I must wait for Sara to connect back with me for pick-up and confirmation. The rain had ended, so to kill some time, I peeked at the wooded area around me. I walk about a hundred feet to finally notice a clear view of the venue where this, whatever the hell it was, just happened. It is a very beautiful building, has a part-church, part-community center appearance to it. A long trail goes to a small area with one-room cabins, another goes directly to Dan's home – A three-level mansion that even in Berlin Georgia would be worth well into seven figures! I continue to walk through the woods, primarily just killing time, when something catches my eye.

A clearing about another fifty feet inland. I walk over to it. I find that it was altered in some way. Like something was either being evaluated for something or was modified altogether. I walk around a bit and see two areas roughly about ten feet in length that appear like holes were dug and then filled in. I looked around some more to see if something else was in this area. It is desolate. Dan's compound was the only thing for miles it seems. My mind starts to overthink about nothing. I proceed to return to the 'outhouse'. Go back in, I realize that I haven't eaten all day. Just as I am wondering if I need to head back out and forage, Sara returns, a little out of breath.

"What did you think?" She smiles.

"I have no idea what that was. Are all of these 'Ritual' things the same?"

"Pretty much, except we haven't had Ali in one of these in a while."

"She looked miserable, as always."

"That's the way Dan likes her. He has told me on more than one occasion that her personality is perfect for what he needs her to do."

"What, be a clueless bitch?"

"More like bitch! He doesn't think she is clueless by a long shot."

"I am sorry, Sara, I need to eat. Can we get out of here?"

"Yes, but first, we have to take this thing down, I don't want anyone stumbling onto the 'outhouse!'"

"OK, that is fine, let's just make it quick. I am about to start eating the mushrooms and berries in the forest here."

Chapter 38

We tore down the structure and spread the fragments under leaves and other various spots far from the fence of the compound. We had to hustle. Sara needed to be back in her cabin on the property before anyone knew she was gone. We began the ride back, and I was curious about a few things.

"Sara. I have been thinking a lot about this "Indoctrination" stuff. How come you didn't fall for it."

She glanced at me and I could tell she wanted to formulate an answer that encompassed her feelings. "I didn't know at first. When I met Dan, I was so lost and still in a ton of pain from my 'Sambies' dying. I think I still had some serious issues with God and why He took them from me, that is why I was always cautious."

"Sambies?" I tried not to chuckle.

"Yes, Sambies – Sam and Sam Jr. They were my team."

"I know," I said and tapped her shoulder.

"Anyway, my parents always gave me a hard time because I questioned everything. From the time I was a little girl, I never took anything at face value. I would let people and things do what they do until my suspicions are proved wrong. Dan never proved me wrong. Plus, the night at the hotel put me in a completely different mindset about him, Comptor, and Proverbs."

"I wish I had that ability. I always gave people the benefit of the doubt until it was too late. I would be perfect cult material."

"Aeron don't say that. You have a good heart. I have no suspicions about you. I knew the moment I met you that I could trust you."

"Thanks, Sara, I haven't heard something like that in a long time." We looked at each other, smiled, and she turned into the motel parking lot.

We got up to the room. She had to gather a few more things before heading back. I knew I needed another shower but wanted to wait until she left. I sat on the bed and watched her pack.

"Do we have a plan for tomorrow?"

"Well, I am going to work. You need to lay low until I get back here when we talk to Joanie, she is getting here at about five. She texted me earlier, she seems to have a few interesting leads."

"Yes, Ma'am," I saluted as a goof.

She looked at me for a longer period than normal. I could feel her stare at me.

"Aeron, why did your ex-wife leave you?"

I sat up, not expecting that question. "Wow, zingers before heading out the door...I guess like in a lot of marriages people just grow apart."

"Why do you think that is?"

"I really don't know. That is what still haunts me. She just didn't want to be married to me anymore. Marriage counseling, praying, begging, nothing worked. She just wanted out."

"Did you want out?"

"No, not ever."

"Do you think she thinks of you at all?"

"No."

"Do you still think of her?"

"Yes, all the time...Why are you asking me this, Sara."

"This may sound strange because I don't know you all that well, but I don't understand how someone could just leave you. You just ooze loyalty. I see how you have embraced everything I have done with all of this since we met."

"Loyalty isn't love, Sara."

"Well, in my world it is, and I appreciate it."

"Thanks, I think you have somewhere to be." I winked.

She finished leaving with me lying on the bed. I had a lot to think about for the remainder of the night.

I took an extremely long shower. Did not want to be alone tonight. Sara's presence was something I was becoming more accustomed to. I missed her the moment I went back to bed. I wanted to reach out to her but did not. I always appreciate proper etiquette. Not being creepy is a good motto for us old guys to stick to when dealing with a younger woman. I knew Sara was an old soul but didn't want to make my assumptions. I have a hard time trusting my instincts these days. I decided to lay back and just channel surf for a while. I longed to be able to fall asleep. CNN, Me TV, PBS, ESPN all the alphabet soup as I surf. My mind continues to race. I had no booze to soothe me and did not have the energy to venture out. I tried to meditate, muscle relaxation, mental health exercises...Roseanne was failing me, or I was just failing myself. I figured the best bet was to just try and sleep. I rolled over, hugged a pillow, and hoped for the best.

I hovered about twenty feet in the air, my eyes opened, and I was getting bearings. As I looked around this, all was so familiar. The staircase, the hallways, the living room. I saw Aeron on the couch, with the dog, watching TV. I turned to my right, the backdoor to the yard. The left, kitchen, dining room. I did not have a chance to take it all in when the front door opened, I watched Aeron leaving the couch and making a beeline for the door. I heard Aeron from below, "Buffy, Mommy's home!! Go see your Mama." Aeron told the dog. She entered the house, Trek bike in tow. Aeron grabbed it from her like he had so many nights before. She had a long day of work and Cross Fit training. She looks exhausted, but also funny. Not a look that Tara would usually have. Aeron scrambled the bike to the back-yard terrace. She was hugging Buffy. From above, I loved watching these two beautiful blonds. My Blondie and our blond Labrador. It was what I lived for. She stood up, much more serious. Aeron knew there was something wrong. "Tara, are you OK, what is it, something happened at work today?" Aeron stood not thinking anything other than the world just sucks and his sweet baby was treated like garbage again. She just looked at Aeron. She put her head down and walked to our breakfast bar. As I was watching this from above, I knew what was coming. I was getting sick. Aeron, from below, did not yet. Aeron sauntered to the other side that led into our kitchen. They stood face to face across the breakfast bar. A very Clint Eastwood-type spaghetti western moment. She pulled her pistol first. "I am not happy... We need to talk to someone." I was watching Aeron and feeling myself above the room. My spirit knew what was happening, but Aeron was just getting the news for the first time. He failed just as I did years earlier. Blindsided "What did I do?" I didn't want to hear Tara's responses, I already knew what they were. "I don't know if I love you anymore." All I wanted was out of this. I knew the ending or at least the spirit in this dream knew the outcome. I wish I could have taken Aeron by the scruff of the neck. Get him out of that kitchen and bring him to my level. Aeron's life was over as he knew it. I had no control from above.

My eyes opened, I was sweaty and, damn it, wet pants! At least I pissed myself when Sara wasn't in the room. That was a gift in itself. I just sighed and laid back for a moment. I am still so fucked up. No one can save me.

Chapter 39

I received a text around 8:30 am. "Laura is here this week, too. Looks like she is helping get Ali set up and settled in here."

I respond, "Great, the 'intern' and the 'hamster' are together again...LOL." "You are going to have to give me more details on those nicknames at some point ☺" she answered back and followed. "Stay close to the room, I am going to try and get out here earlier so we can meet with Joanie, she really has a lot to tell us." "OK, I will stay put."

I decided to try to get more research done on Dan and Comptor's business dealings. I was very curious about the bankruptcy, and how we were the "so-called" reason for it. I went into the bankruptcy case which was provided through public records. Looks like he had less than a million dollars in assets and nearly 10 million dollars in debt. I went back to our financials from that year, and we were still less than a 5-million-dollar company, soup to nuts. I can see that we may have taken a few accounts that he bid on, but there is no way we were the reason for the bankruptcy. He just seems like a horrible businessman in general. He has risky investments, bad decisions, and, from what I have noticed in my own dealings, very incompetent people, he puts in prominent roles. The lack of accountability and judgment is shocking. He blamed Alec for his company going under when all he had to do was look in the mirror. I am not much of a mental health expert, but I see some narcissistic qualities in him, along with terrible business communication skills.

After a few hours of this, I need to take a walk. I endeavor out to the motel parking lot and head off to a convenience store down the street for a snack. I walk into the store and see an old man at the counter, the kind of guy who was born, raised, and grew up in Berlin. I grab a 5-hour energy, granola bar, and ask "Hey, do you carry Kombucha in here?" "Kom what??" he said. "Never mind." I just add an unsweetened iced tea to my haul and go to pay.

"You're not from here, are you mister?"

"No, just here for a few days on business."

"Do you work for that Comptor place?"

"No, not work for them but have had some business dealings."

"Can't stand that guy who runs it. That Dan whatever his name is."

"Really, what's his problem?"

"What isn't...Since he took over the city council, he got rid of all us locals who run the systems in town. He put all these young chicks in these positions. I ran the tax assessment office for twenty years and he fired me two years ago and changed the property tax structure. All went up like we live in some big city or something. He wants to run all of us out of town!"

"How do you think he has been able to do that?"

"He has money and that's all you need. I am barely hanging on to this store, now. This place has been in the family for fifty years, I am on the verge of selling. We hear his next big project is taking on real estate and building up downtown with condominiums or some other bullshit. The rest of us are goners if that happens."

"I have heard that crime is real low in town."

"Hardly, where did you hear that? Things happen all the time, they just get swept away. He appointed a female sheriff and all women deputies too. They harass every man left in this town."

"What about the church thing I hear about?"

"There are none anymore. He got rid of the two Christian churches we had in town and put something on his damn property that no local is allowed to go to. I hear it is all women too. Me and fellas talk that he is trying to create a city of all women. Such a weirdo!"

"I have done business with him for years and never heard of this before."

"If I were you, whatever business you are doing, find someone else. I wouldn't trust that guy as far as I could throw him."

"Enlightening, Thanks. What do I owe you?"
"$8.67."

I handed him a 10 and told him to keep the change and appreciate the information. He smiles, salutes, and I walk out. Heading back to the motel, the information is flowing in my head. If Dan can take over this town and build real estate, his empire will be able to expand to other cities and churches and continue to fortify this cult he has created. I wonder how much of this Sara knows. Dan betrayed the people of this town, as well as everything else he had done.

I get back to the room and Sara texts that she is on her way back. She is meeting Joanie and they will both come up together. "Give me half an hour," she texts. I pop the 5-hour energy, munch on the bar, and wash it down with the iced tea. The caffeine is flowing, and I am ready for the next phase of the plan.

Sara and Joanie walk into the room, halfway in conversation. I am sitting on the bed, legs crossed. I can feel the energy coming out of both. The connection between them is obvious. I brace for who will speak first.

Sara begins, "I don't want to get too far ahead here but Joanie has already given me some flavor of what we are dealing with."

"I got some information to share with you guys, too."

"OK, great, I will let Joanie get started and we will move on from there." Sara was the ringmaster of the information to come.

Joanie started. It was hard to keep up at first. She was ready to burst. I can see her reporter sensibility taking over. She may have the story of a lifetime here. She can hardly keep her skin from peeling off.

She started explaining that the two employees, Sophie Novak and Kim Fried, were missing persons. She spoke to Sophie's parents and Kim's brother. They had become disillusioned with what Dan and Proverbs were doing and wanted out. Both had discussed with family about leaving. Kim's brother talked about how she had discovered information about the bad business practices of Comptor and some issues with the locals. She was attempting to get some other people involved. Sophie and Kim were friends working together to gather information to incriminate Dan and his team. Both Sophie and Kim's family corroborated that the last time they spoke to them. Which was on the same day, last April. Kim's brother told me she told him, "I think I found the smoking gun of what he is doing. I just need a few more days to confirm it." That was the last anyone heard from her. Joanie checked cell phone records and bank transactions for both and nothing. The families never suspected Dan because he donated money to help the effort for both families in the missing person search. He did this somewhat discreetly and didn't want fanfare for it and asked both families to keep it to themselves.

I asked the first question, "So Dan knew they were both missing, tried to help, but didn't want any pub for it?"

"Exactly. Strange, right?"

"Very"

I then thought about what I found in the woods the day before and explained to both how I stumbled onto a clearing close to the 'outhouse' set up and two areas that I now believe could possibly be graves.

Sara spoke up, "You mean gravesites? People?"

"That is what it looked like to me. I am no expert on that, but when both my parents died and I went to fresh burials, it looked similar to that."

"Two of them?"

"Yes."

Joanie chimed in, "Were these on the property?"

"No, about 300-500 feet from the fencing. I was just wandering around killing time until Sara picked me up."

Sara and Joanie looked at each other, Sara spoke, "We got to go out there right now, this has gone to a whole different level!"

"OK, I am driving?"

"Easy, there guy, I got this." Sara took over as she did.

We headed out, and I took the time to explain what I had found out with the research and the old man at the convenience store.

"No matter what, we have to take care of this, now. Time is not on our side here!" Sara was concise and determined.

Joanie made her statement. "I am going to call a guy at the FBI that I have worked with before. We need someone down here. This is bigger than all of us. When are you done on the compound, Sara?"

"Friday."

"OK, wheels in motion after we get back!"

We arrive at the same spot that started this on Sunday. I walked them both to the clearing and showed what I suspected were the two graves.

"We don't have shovels, so what do we do?" Sara asked.

"We are not going to dig this up, Sara," I noted.

Joanie brought clarity, "I will get the FBI agent I know involved. He can have a team down here and they will monitor the area. Eventually, they will dig this up. Hopefully, it is just some broken-hearted kids' pets buried down there."

"OK, sorry, I am a little on edge right now!" Sara was salty and resolved.

We spent a few more minutes at the site, made the way back to the car, then the motel. It was dusk and we were all tired. Joanie had rented a room in the motel and headed back to hers. It was just me and Sara and I felt at ease with her, even with all the tension and stress that was enveloping both of us. We ordered a pizza —

tried to calm the nerves. We needed to focus on what was next.

"Sara, do we just let the FBI and Joanie handle this? It seems like we have some probable cause to at least start an investigation, and get the newspapers involved."

"No, I don't trust that, at all. I need to get something concrete, on tape. Can we set up some sort of sting?"

"Sting? You mean try to get Dan to say something?"

"Yeah, I can have a wire and meet with him and see if I can get him to admit to something. He has told me about a lot over the last year."

"Sara, come on, that is quite an ask. Plus, what if he is on to you? I am seeing some sociopathic qualities about him, and he is sorta paranoid. If you are in that compound, and he has killed people before, I wouldn't want you to be anywhere near that."

"Aeron, I am fine, I can handle myself."

"I know you can, but do you really need to, in this case? There are people good at this shit and can do it themselves."

I was selfish, of course. I was catching feelings for Sara and didn't want anything to happen to her. I may be falling for her. I continue to fight it.

"When we meet with Joanie tomorrow, we will figure some things out."

Chapter 40

We both slept together again. Back-to-back. It felt so good. I awoke a few times during the night and just enjoyed hearing her breath. It took everything I had to not touch her, cuddle her, spoon her. I had no dreams. I felt safe just in her presence. Sara is one of the most extraordinary women who had come into my life in a long time. I knew I could not tell her that. Inside me I felt something I had not for years. I did not want to let her down. I knew she needed me to help her, and my obligation was to fulfill whatever she thought I could do. This journey we were on was for me, too. I believe Sara knew that. Probably more than I. So much to excise. I lay next to her, knowing all of that. I formulate how I will thank her for everything she has done for me. Sara is saving me. If I walked away now, she would still have saved me. Gave me something to be passionate about again. To tap into skills no one else cared about. I was worthy. I lift my hand to just touch her on the shoulder. I come within inches and pull back. Not appropriate. I just grab a pillow and squeeze it extra tight. Roll over to my side, look at the wall, and try to get a few more minutes of shut-eye. We have so much to do, and I cannot wait for Sara to give me the direction I need to move forward.

She wakes up first and nudges me. I hug the pillow tight and smile. I hear her voice on top of me.

"Hey there, sleepy. Wake up. We have a big day ahead."

I roll over and just look at her. She is the most beautiful person. I would not want to be anywhere else than right here.

"I am awake. Need coffee, now." I give her a goofy look; she responds with her signature smile.

"On it." She heads out of the room, and I start to get my bearings.

I give a big sigh and start to brace for what is going to be another epic day in this trek. I have not fully come to comprehend what is happening around me. I am a bit of a reluctant warrior in this adventure. I have an opinion of Dan... spoiler, I hate him. He took my life from me, yet I see Sara, and the passion she feels is something I have yet to totally understand. Being a man may be my first problem. I do know Sara has experienced things I have never experienced before. My dumb ass better get on the same page, understanding or not. If she needs me to help her, I know it will help me. I keep reinforcing that in the minutes before she comes back into the room. She arrives with two 24-ounce coffees, some bagel sandwiches, and an extra donut for me. She is smart enough to know that I need a little extra to get going in the morning.

"Joanie is on her way over, and she has an agent from the FBI that wants to talk to all of us."

"I guess we needed that at some point. Is he going to be with her or virtual?"

"Virtual, dummy, it is 2023."

Joanie raps on the door, and Sara lets her in. She walks over to the table and pulls her computer out.

"I am going to introduce you guys to someone I have worked with in the past. Anytime I need to get the feds involved, he is the first one I call. His name is Special Agent Tom Bridges. Let me just make sure the Wi-Fi is good here. I have to set up this adaptor on my computer to make the Wi-Fi restricted. We don't want anyone eavesdropping." She smiles.

"I am glad all of you know this IT stuff. I am completely lost with the tech you use." I stated.

"It isn't that difficult, dude." Joanie comes off a little miffed at me, and rightfully so.

Joanie gets everything set up, and we hang around the computer screen as Tom comes on. He certainly looks the part. Black sports jacket, white shirt, black tie. Perfect military crew cut. Looks around my age. I figured he was a lifer. I am sure it is a great career. I wouldn't know about that anymore. Joanie gets us up to speed on the relationship she has with Tom, then he discusses his background. He takes over the conversation from there.

"With everything Joanie has told me, we are still trying to discern what our role in this will be going forward. This may be a more appropriate situation for the local authorities in Berlin."

I shut that down. "That will probably not be an option, Mr. Bridges. I spoke to a local yesterday who filled in a lot of the internal government workings here, and Dan Rand is the head of the city council. He pretty much makes every key decision in this town now. He appointed the sheriff himself."

"OK, then we will need something concrete before I can move my team in. Especially with these two missing women. I can come down and get the Georgia Bureau involved, but you got to give me something."

We all take a pause and look at each other. I looked down at Tom, and I knew we were not going to get an idea from his side. Sara makes her pitch.

"What if I get Dan to admit that he killed them?"

I look over at her, eyes squinted, "Get him to admit to the murders? Sara, you are kidding, right?"

"No, I am not. Look, I am out of here at the end of the week. I can call a meeting with him, we can put a wire on me, and I can get it out of him."

"No, Sara, that is way too risky. What if he suspects something? You are on that compound, and we won't be able to get you out." I implore my concern.

Tom interjects, "Well, if she thinks she can get a confession out of him, I can have a team ready to storm the compound and get him and get her out. Look, we can put together a case for blackmail, bribery, possibly find fraud, and money laundering, but to take the entire organization down, if these two women were murdered by him or people within his circle. Game over."

"I can do it," Sara stated confidently.

"Sara, no, no. There has to be another way."

"Aeron, there is no other way."

Joanie responds, "Tom will have a team here, and we can get her if it gets hairy. Any confession from him, and this whole thing blows up. That's what we want, right? Sara told me what that bastard did to you and her."

"Yes, I know, but I just don't want her to be in danger."

"Aeron, I have to do this." She takes my hand. "Look at me, I have to do this."

I looked into her eyes, conceded, and we moved on.

Tom takes the lead. "OK, I will get on the horn with the GA Bureau in Savannah, and we will start to put together a team of 4-6 agents to get out there. Sara when can you meet with him?"

"I will set it up for Thursday."

"Perfect, Joanie, let's meet up later today, and I will give you all the logistics. Sara, we will provide you with the wire and have that put on you the morning of the meeting."

"That sounds great. I will be ready."

I sit on the bed as the three of them finish up the meeting. My mind is racing. Anxiety is bubbling back to a place I had not felt since Sara and I began this journey. Joanie packs her computer and lets us know she will be in touch after she and Tom get the details worked out. It is me and Sara alone in the room.

"I am sorry, Aeron."

"Sorry? You don't need to be sorry. I just don't understand why you feel like you need to do this."

"I know how I can get him to talk."

"Please, explain."

"I can't. You will know when you listen."

"Cryptic, not helpful."

"All I want you to do for me is trust me. We are going to take him down. I have been working on this for a year. I have been waiting for this ever since he had me in that motel room in Tallahassee."

"You don't need revenge, Sara."

"I don't want revenge. I want justice. Not just for me, but for every woman he has lied to, manipulated, and now, from what we think, killed."

"You don't have to take this entire fight on your own."

"I am not, and I have you to help me. I needed you, and you came through. I just need you now to stay focused, and let's get this done together."

She grabs me and pulls me in for a hug. I didn't want to let her go. I had not felt safe for so long. Being in Sara's arms is a place I could live. She kisses me on the cheek, and we both lie down for a nap. My emotions are running so high, my bearings need to be centered. No wallowing. I just wish I knew what Sara's plan was to get Dan to talk. She is full of surprises; I am sure she has a few more for all of us.

Chapter 41

Sara wakes up after a few hours. She needs to head back to the compound for the night. We have less than 48 hours before her meeting with Dan. We have no plan or idea of what will happen, no tangible help. What could go wrong?

"How are you going to set this up, Sara?"

"I have a meeting with Dan, Ali, and Laura at 11 am. We are starting to discuss our transition. After the meeting is over, I am going to ask him for a private meeting the next day. Sort of a goodbye lunch. I want to "Thank him" for everything he has done for me while at the compound.""

"My anxiety goes through the roof just thinking about this."

"Well, you need to stop that. Turn the dial down. I know what I am doing."

"Sara...How in the hell are you going to get him to admit what happened to those two women?"

"I will, just trust me." She winks and heads for the door. "I am not going to see you again until after the meeting with Dan, so if this all goes well, I will let you buy me a drink."

"So, what do I do for the next day and a half."

"Do you knit?"

"Funny, Sara. What are we going to do after all of this is done?"

Sara relaxes for a minute and contemplates the question. Her head rises, and she smiles that sweet Sara smile before responding.

"How about I let you take the wheel on that? I think I have made enough decisions lately."

"Deal, I will come up with something... You better come back to me, kiddo."

"Deal." She winks and walks out of the room.

I am preparing for what could be the longest wait I have dealt with for years. So many thoughts rush through me. I went back to sitting in the waiting room of my marriage counselor's office week after week while Tara was making her way from work for our sessions. I was Preparing to be obliterated again. Those 10-15 minutes in that lobby felt like being led off to slaughter. I guess the stakes are a lot higher now. Being hammered about why your wife doesn't love you anymore seems trivial compared to a woman being put in a position to either save the world or lose her own life. Perspective is something I have struggled with. Part of being the emotional wreck that I am. I am going to dig deep and be what Sara needs me to be. She has given me back purpose, and I will do whatever I have to do to help her, protect her, and save her like she has me. I don't know if I can do that, but she deserves the best that I got. I hope it is enough. I kill a few hours overthinking and overstimulating before falling asleep. The hours are going to feel like wading through mud.

I sleep surprisingly well. No dreams, no issues. I checked the phone, and Sara had already set up a video call with Tom and Joanie. She set it for her lunch hour at

1 pm. All I can do is wait or make my way back to the convenience store for coffee. Probably not the best idea. I will see if there is any luck in the motel office. Maybe get some reading material, as well.

I walk down to the motel office. Fortunately for me, there is a coffee vending machine. Did not think these were still in service. Looks like it could be about 40 years old. I ask the half-catatonic clerk, "Does this thing still work?" he responds, "Yes, but I wouldn't drink that." "Perfect," I speak. I put my two dollars in, and it prepares a 16-ounce cup with cream and sugar. I lift the cup out, and it looks more like tar with some white specs floating around. I take a sip, "I have had worse, not really." I asked the clerk if there was a newspaper machine around. He tells me it is right outside the door, and I would have to be completely blind to miss it. The hospitality on a "hump day" in this town is fabulous. I make my way out to the machine about 10 feet from the front door. I inspected the area to see if I could have missed seeing it to plead my case to the clerk, then thought the better of it and just put my dollar in for a copy. I pull out the paper "The Berlin Femella Weekly," and somehow, I see the continued pattern of this town in that title. I look up "femella" on my phone. Medieval Latin. Female. Great. The headline confirms what the convenience store clerk spoke to me about yesterday: Local Company Ready to Start Building Projects in Town. I skim quickly and read glowing commentary on Comptor and Dan Rand helping to bring Berlin Georgia, back to life. I am sure the entire staff is on his payroll. I walk back to the room and choke down the cup of coffee, continuing to go through the pages of the weekly. The byline for every article is female. I count seven different women who wrote stories on the issue. No male writers and many references to God, church, and even a Dear Abby-style column for advice called "The Divine Femme." Both answers were filled with scripture and fluff that honestly had little to do with the questions the submitter was asking. I crinkle up the paper and plug my computer in. I need a shower before getting set up for the meeting. I try everything to keep my anxiety at a minimum.

Feeling perked up, I set myself up at the table with my legal pad, pen, and a deep breath. This plan is now going to be formed. I am excited to see Sara. She has sub-consciously taken over my headspace, and it feels good. We all get on the call. Tom takes the lead.

"Hey everyone, let me update you on where we are at with the planning. Sara confirmed with Joanie that the meeting with Dan would be at 4:00 pm tomorrow, just the two of them. This will make things easy to get her in and out. We will have a truck about three miles offsite that will be monitoring the wire. Me, a few other federal agents and four GA Bureau agents will be in the truck. I will have backup roughly 10 minutes away if we need re-inforcements."

"Aeron and I will be at the motel monitoring from there. When Sara is done and has her information, she will go straight to her car and leave the property. She will be already packed up, and she will never have to be in that place again." Joanie explains. "I have the story ready to go in the Sunday Post. All I need is for Sara to take care of the smoking gun."

"The story isn't important, Joanie. Getting Sara out of there unscathed. If she can't get him to talk, she just needs to get out of that place. You understand." I implored.

"She will be fine. Sara knows what she is doing."

"Joanie, don't be cavalier with Sara's life, OK. Fuck the damn story. I don't want her going in there at all."

"I am a reporter, Aeron. That is my job. A story is happening no matter what goes on in there."

"I swear to God, if you betray her..."

Sara speaks up, "Guys, relax, stop the bickering. I understand what is at stake here. The story will be done, and I will get the information that we all need to get where we want to go."

I look at Sara on the screen. Tom, visibly annoyed, chimes in, "Excuse me, ladies, can we get back to business here?"

We all agree, and Tom continues.

"I provided a wire for Joanie to give to Sara later tonight. It is very easy to install, clip it into your bra. It is very sensitive and will pick up every damn noise in the room, even a fart. The transmitter is a little tricky. It is the size of a keychain, so she will need to wear slacks and keep it no more than two feet from the mic. I will give Joanie access to the transmission on her computer so they can listen in. There is no camera, so we will not know the logistics of what is going on in that room, unless you keep talking, Sara."

Sara answers, "I understand."

I ask, "If things go bad, do you know where to go on that compound to find her?"

"Good question." Tom smiles. "There is a tracking device in the transmitter, so once she turns it on, we will know exactly where she is. This is why holding on to that transmitter is critical."

Sara responds, "Got it."

Tom finishes the meeting in true FBI fashion. Does another complete rundown of the plan, gives the names of all the agents participating, and wishes everyone good luck. We will all reconvene at 3:30 pm the next day. The call drops. I am about to go into a panic attack, and my phone goes off. It is a text from Sara, "Are you OK? You seem a little worked up." I think for a minute before responding, "Yeah, I am fine. Just never been a part of anything like this before." "Neither have I...LOL." "Yeah...LOL." "Aeron, get some rest. I need you focused tomorrow. I need you ☺" I look at the last text and rub it with my thumb. I see the three words over and over, *I...Need...You.* Why does she have so much faith in me when I don't have faith in myself? This is going to be a very long night.

Chapter 42

The room shrinks, and I am alone at a round table. I don't think I am still in the motel room. It expands, then shrinks again. Each time, a figure appears at the table. I see a silhouette of a body but cannot see the face. This happens 3-4-5 more times. I see silhouettes now encircling the table. The shadows make it impossible to make out anyone. I am bracing for what or who they could be. I have been here before and just want out. I feel a hand on my right shoulder, and the voice tells me not to turn around. It is a female voice; it gives me a slight bit of comfort. The time continues to move. The uneasiness puts me in a position to move, squirm, and want to stand up. The room turns completely black, and then the lights come up. I am blinded for a moment, but when my pupils finally get their orientation, I see the faces. They are all there. The intern, the hamster, Alec, Dan, Mom, Dad, Tara, Clint, and I now see others, more people in my life who have hurt me, used me and betrayed me. They all just stare. I feel the heat of the eyes burning into me. The hand on my shoulder closes onto my traps, and I hear a whisper in my ear. "Rise above them. I need you..." "Sara? Is that you?" "Shhhh. Just look at them, rise above. I need you." "Sara, I can't look at them. They will destroy me." "Be strong, for once, be strong!" "Sara, I need to see you." I turn around and see Sara in a coffin. "Sara!!!!!" her eyes open. "I needed you, and you betrayed me..."

I jerked out of the dream and pissed myself again. I am running out of ways to clean my underwear this week. My gawd. The day has come. I can't hold anything together. I see the sunrise through the curtain. I go to the window; it looks like a beautiful day is about to start. The day of reckoning has arrived. I can't even keep from whizzing my pants. What does Sara need from me? I gave her the information she requested, and now she believes I can help with what is coming today. I just don't understand. I am a mental wreck. Have not had a drink in 6 days, which is a modern-day record. Sara is about to pull one of the bravest acts I will ever witness, and she needs me? I hope I will find some answers.

Chapter 43

To say that I am a nervous wreck is certainly an understatement. I'm not wired for something like this. Eight months ago, I was running operations for a successful regional company. Just trying to get by with my emotional bullshit and planning retirement. Now, I am caught up in a financial blackmail conspiracy scheme with a cult leader looking to expand an empire into something I don't know what. I have found this incredible woman who has changed my entire outlook on life. Now, she is about ready to put her life on the line to try and stop this. As I continue my wallowing merry-go-round, the phone goes off. Text from Sara, "Morning, are you ready?" I respond, "Ready for what?" "For this to all be over." "That is the hope. Just don't do anything crazy, Sara. We have a lot already, just be smart and get out of there." "Don't you worry about me, got it covered ☺" "Sara, we need to talk after this is over. I have so much to say to you. Thinking way too much." "Aeron, we will talk. You will understand everything after today. I promise. Just be strong. I need you." I finish the exchange, taking the high road, "Good Luck, I will be there for you, I promise." I sat on the bed, legs crossed and staring at our exchange. Scrolling up from the beginning and analyzing every word. What is she trying to accomplish today? What will I understand? Why does she need me so much? I need to get coffee and try to move the clock to 4:00 pm. I hope to go to bed tonight, change, and be able to move on. Have to get Sara through this day.

I make my way to the office more than once, coffee after coffee. Pace around the room, around the building. Stare at the clock and try to sleep. No luck. Joanie texted me that she would arrive at the room at 3:00 pm. We have a final meeting with Tom, and he will give us his game plan. I get a little lunch, a waste of time. Cannot eat. Slam two more 5-hour energies. My heart probably is not happy with that, but I will get over it. I know the family history of arrhythmia, but considering where I was just a few weeks ago, the elevated heart rate is the least of my worries. The knock on the door finally arrives. The sight of Joanie is a relief. We are getting closer to getting Sara home.

"Hey Aeron, how are you holding up?"

"Been better. When are we talking to Tom?"

"In about 15 minutes, have you been in touch with Sara today?"

"Yes, we texted this morning. She is ready...More ready than me."

"I know. She seems at peace with all of this. She is one strong girl."

"Was she like this in school?"

"She was always an old soul type; I was drawn to her early on and could not figure out why."

"She has quite a will about her. It is hard not to follow her."

"Yeah, I remember when she and Sam first got together, they were so passionate about making the world a better place. Damn, they just had so much integrity. She questioned everything."

"What were they like?"

"Her and Sam?"

"Yeah."

"Amazing…Never seen two people so in tune with each other."

"He was a good guy?"

"Yeah, Sam was the best. He loved her so much."

"I kind of figured that. I cannot imagine the devastation of losing him."

"And Sam, Jr… We didn't talk for a long time after it all went down. I was shocked when she called me about the Comptor thing. She must have been in a real bad place to get caught up with this crap. Like Sara, she always finds a way to make it right."

"Joanie, what is she going to do today?"

She paused for a moment, "Make it right. That is what she does."

"What the hell does that mean?"

"She is full of surprises. I wouldn't bet against her, yet I couldn't tell you what she will do."

"Can she get him to admit to the murders?"

"If anybody can, she can. Stop worrying. We have the FBI and GBI here, and more than 30 officers are on call. Tom is the best there is at this stuff. She will be fine."

I wish the conversation helped, but it did not ease my mind or heart. I think about Sam and what an incredible person he was for her. To have him, for both to have each other. How she was able to climb out of that emotional abyss and deal with Dan Rand's manipulation. I am in awe of this woman. Joanie snaps me out of it. We get ready for the prep call with Tom. She sets up the video, and it is the three of us and two of Tom's top agents. He leads this, and we don't have much to say. This is his show now.

"Thanks, everyone. We are ready to roll, and just let me brief you on a few things as we get ready. I have six agents in the truck with me. I have put three others in the field about fifty feet from the entrance of the compound. They are armed but will not make any entry unless the whole team is dispatched. The GBI has twenty-one officers and agents a mile outside of town and can be ready to storm the compound in about seven minutes."

I meekly ask, "And Sara?"

"Getting to that." He responds, "Our main in is Sara O'Connor. She has a precise 4:00 pm meeting with the principal at hand, Dan Rand. She will be checking in with us in about three minutes. We can only hear her. We cannot transfer any information through the wire. Joanie Woodard has created a system if we have issues on our end. She will text if we lose contact or if she just needs to bail out."

"What is the system, Tom, if I may ask?"

He seems irritated but responds, "Joanie should have already told you, but obviously she didn't, so if we lose contact, she texts her twice back-to-back. If she needs to bail out, Joanie just texts continuously. The vibrate will let her know to find any means to get out of there."

As he finishes, Sara connects on the video call. She is in her room on the compound.

"Hello everyone." Her smiling face comes up on the call. I am totally fixated on her.

Tom kicks in immediately, "Hello Sara, just briefing the group on the plan. We have timed this out together. You have 23 minutes to get the information before we feel he will start to be suspicious. Set your phone to vibrate before going into the meeting. You know the text codes. We have your back on every level here. If you feel early on that this isn't going to happen, I have three of my guys right outside the front gate. You just need to get off the compound, and we will get you to safety."

"I am ready. I am not leaving until we get what we need."

I nearly walked over her last statement, "Sara, just stick to the plan, please. You don't have to be a hero. You have done enough." Joanie grabs my forearm. "Sara, please, just be smart."

"I am fine, and we are going to get what we need. I know what I am doing."

I clench my fist, and Joanie squeezes my arm even tighter. It was a cue to shut up.

"Thank you, Sara. Game time, folks. We will stay on the video with the group." Tom finishes.

I look at Sara, wanting her to make eye contact with me. She does. I feel her through the screen. All I see in her eyes is, "I need you." We have less than fifteen minutes before the meeting, she falls off. My head sinks into my chest. What do I do?

Chapter 44

I count every second until 4:00 pm. Joanie is sitting at the table in the room. She moved it enough for me to have my small piece of three feet to pace behind her. The curtains are drawn. Clouds have taken over the day. We have one light on the far side of the bed that gives an eerie glow to the room. We heard Sara enter the room and take a seat. Waiting for Dan. The room is a general place for smaller meetings. This is in a separate building from his house and the main auditorium for larger get-togethers. Sara explained this is where most of the blackmail meetings on the compound took place. Rumor was that Dan videoed them all, but no evidence of that has been found yet. Only the video with Alec existed. If we only had all those other videos, maybe Sara would not be in this place today. Dan enters the room. Sara rises from her seat.

"Hi Sara, so good to get together with you today." The rustling tells me they embraced.

"Hi Dan, busy week. We are taking care of a lot for the transition."

"Yes, yes, we are, just give me a few. We have company for this meeting today."

"Company?" Sara is surprised.

"Yes, Ali and Laura will be joining us today."

My heart sinks. I hold my tongue but do not know for how long.

"Ohhh, good. I know we all probably have a lot to work out before I leave tomorrow." Sara adjusts to the changes.

The "intern" and the "hamster" walk into the room, and they all exchange pleasantries. Dan then goes into one of his 'prayers.'

"Before we start today. I am so blessed and want to share something I saw from an amazing female author today, 'Once we start to work with Feminine power, we begin to see that it is not our minds that are in control of this power – it ebbs and flows with the movements of the planets, the procession of the seasons, the moons and tides, our own internal cycles of menstrual, anniversaries, the events around us' Isn't that glorious?" His voice is so proud of himself.

The "intern" and "hamster" respond immediately in unison, "So glorious, Dan, so much." Sara is silent.

Dan questions, "Sara, wasn't that just beautiful? I found that today, actually, just before I came into the room. It is like a sign." He smiles. "Let's all hold hands."

I figured they all took hands, and Dan went into another one of his diatribes, "The deep Feminine, the mystery of consciousness, she who is life, is longing for our transformation as much as we are. She holds back, allowing us free reign to choose, nudging us occasionally with synchronicities, illness, births, and deaths... But when we make space for her, she rushes into all the gaps, engulfing us with her desire for life and expression." I had concluded this wasn't anything original, just some bullshit he found either in a book or on the internet, but he expressed it from the heart. I am sure the congregation will hear this at some point in the future.

The "intern" and "hamster" responded again. "Thank you, Dan. You see the power in us no one else does."

Sara attempts to break them out of the spell, "That is wonderful, Dan, but I called this meeting to discuss some things with you."

"Certainly, Sara, please, what is on your mind. Ali and Laura, take the seats directly behind me."

I would give anything to be in that room. Hearing this with no video is just so...

"Dan, we have worked together for quite a while, and I have been on the compound for over a year now. This does feel like home to me, but I have some concerns I want to discuss with you before I exit tomorrow."

"Concerns?"

"Yes, Dan, I want to..."

He interrupts her, "Sara, are you talking about the transfer? This has been in the works for a while. You are going to be instrumental in our next merger. You are meeting with the head of Universe Corp. in Tallahassee, Clayton Morgan, next Tuesday. I have told him about you. I believe he knows you. You are going to help us close this deal."

"Dan, I know Mr. Morgan. Two of my best friends interned at his company when I was in college. He knows my father."

"Even better, this could be the biggest acquisition yet... he is still on the fence. We just need to push it over."

"Dan, before we go forward, I just have a question for you?"

"Sure, Sara, anything."

"What happened to Sophie and Kim?"

"Sophie and Kim?" He pauses for a moment. "They left the company?"

"Are you sure, Dan?"

I stop in my tracks and grab Joanie, "What is she doing!!" Joanie responds, "Getting the truth." I pull Joanie out of her seat, "This isn't the plan!!"

Sara continues, "Dan, I am just trying to protect you. I have heard some things that maybe they disappeared. You know how some like to snoop around."

"Sara, rumors are just what men do to keep everyone down."

"What if a woman gets the information, Dan?"

I again implore to no avail, "What the hell is she doing!!!"

"Dan, those women, they died, didn't they?" a silence ensues. We all are frozen in our space.

Dan sighs, "Sara, you are too curious sometimes."

Sara then blurts out, "I know about Alec."

"Alec."

"The video, Dan. I found it."

"The video? Ali, do you know about this?"

Ali states, "Yes, the video we showed Alec that closed the Vivant deal, that was deleted a long time ago."

"Ali, no, it wasn't. I saw it." I can feel Sara staring at her even without seeing her.

"I showed it to Aeron, Dan."

"Aeron? You mean that minion who worked at Vivant?"

"Yeah, and he gave me all the information I need to see what this company is doing."

"Huh...Sara, what are you talking about?"

"That's not important, Dan. It is just us now."

I started screaming at Tom. "Get her out of there, pull the cord, Tom. Get her out of there!!"

Tom stays stoic, "Just a few more minutes, he may confess. Just be patient."

I scream again, "Tom!!!! No, fuck this, get her out of there, now."

Sara continues, "Dan, you raped me in that motel room, and I know you killed those two, and I am here to take you down."

Dan gets up out of his seat, puts his forefinger over his mouth, waits, and looks over at Ali and Laura. "Looks like we have a problem here, Sara, don't we?"

"I have no problem, Dan. I just want to make sure we get all of this out before you send me on my next mission."

"Well, looks like plans have changed a bit, haven't they? I know you are not bright enough to bring in anyone else. How much does Aeron know?"

I again beg with Tom, "Get her out of there."

He replies, "Not yet!"

I say, "Fuck this, I am going to get her, now!!"

Joanie tries to grab me, "No, Aeron, we are almost there."

I grab Joanie's car keys off the table, "Fuck you all, don't betray Sara. I am getting her now."

I have nothing to access her. All I could do was drive to the compound. I can be there in less than seven minutes. I jumped in Joanie's Honda CRV and pushed the pedal to the floor as far as it could go, and I wished it would have gone through the floor. I get to the gate of the compound and just drive right through. In the rearview, I see two of the agents with rifles come out of hiding. No help from them. I have no bearings about me. I see the auditorium and the house. I just want to find Sara. On my right, I see figures moving: three women. That is what I am looking for. I stopped the vehicle and started running toward the figures. The compound is so enclosed that no way out is possible. That is to my advantage. I ran like the Olympic 100-meter final was in my grasp. Then, the gunshot. I stop and start again. I know where the sound came from: behind the auditorium. My phone went off. Too much to multitask. I come around the south end of the auditorium. I see the "intern," gun in hand. I run and lunge at her. The gun goes off. It leaves her hand. I am on top of her from behind. She is struggling, trying to fight me. I turn her over. She scratches at my face; I get her hands under control. Pinned behind her head. I am straddling her. She has a look in her eye of utter contempt and crazy toward me. I look to my right and see Sara. I see the blood, her body struggling. I scream, "Sara!!" I continue to hold the "intern." The power of the cult is raging through her veins. I am her ultimate enemy. The agents arrived and pulled me off her. I struggle. I want Sara. I take my phone out of my pocket and see just three words from Joanie: "We Got Him!!" I throw the phone to the ground, crawl over to Sara, and pull her into my arms.

"What took you so long?" She laughs while struggling to breathe.

"Ahh, had my hands full."

"Did you hear? We got him. He admitted to the killings."

"No, I was trying to save you."

"Aeron, I don't need to be saved. This is what was supposed to happen."

"What do you mean?"

"This was what I wanted all along."

"I don't understand, Sara."

"You don't have to, Aeron. All you need to know is that without you, this wouldn't have been able to happen."

"Sara?"

"Aeron, I am going home now. I am going to be with my Sambies again. We are going to be a family. That is all I want. I just needed to do a few more things before I left. I needed to make things right in the world, and I became enamored with you. You have been through so much and been hurt by so many. I just wanted to make things right by you, too. This is why I needed you. I just want you to do one thing for me."

"Anything, Sara."

"Live, just live, and find happiness. You deserve it so much. I promise we will look over you. You are a good man; don't ever forget that." She squeezes my hand; I look into her eyes, and she goes limp. I bring her to my chest and hold her like the whole world is in my hands.

Chapter 45

I hold Sara for what feels like an eternity. Joanie comes to me and breaks the moment.

"They need to take her now." She touches my shoulder.

"I know. I just can't let her go."

"Aeron, it is okay. She will be in good hands."

I let go of my grip on her, stood up, and tried to compose myself. I have been oblivious to what is going on around me. The "intern" and "hamster" are handcuffed face down on the grass. I see what looks like dozens of agents on the grounds. Tom Bridges approaches me. "Can you take me to the clearing?" I respond, "Yes," yet cannot stop staring at the "intern" on the grass. I slowly walk over to her, stand over her for a moment, get down on one knee, and just wait for her to make eye contact. It takes a bit, but when she does. That is all I need. "Ali, we all own you now." The disdain on her face gives me the satisfaction I am looking for. I got up, and Joanie led me out of the compound. I stared at the "intern" the entire way. I wanted her to feel my despise.

I exit the compound, and we make our way to the clearing. This is where we all feel are the graves of Sophie and Kim. That confirmation would come later. My catatonic state cannot be broken. Still processing that Sara is gone. Joanie and I walked back to her SUV, and we made our way back to the motel. I look out the window and see the wilderness pass. The trees, shrubs, billboards, it is all there and all empty. The short time that Sara was in my life felt like a lifetime. Joanie breaks the silence.

"She was amazing...You did everything you could."

"Except save her..."

"Look, Aeron. I have known her for a long time. Sara gets an idea in her head, and she runs with it. When she contacted me, I had never seen her more determined."

"I am sure."

"The information she gave us top to bottom is going to take this guy and his warped ideas down. It is over now."

"She didn't have to die."

"Yeah, I know... I hate to say it, but this is what she wanted."

I open my mouth to object and put my fist over my mouth instead, "I know." I concede.

"I promise you, the story I put out tomorrow is going to blow the doors off everyone. I recommend that when you connect with any of your business contacts back home, all hell is going to break loose."

"That's probably not a bad idea. Joanie, can I ask you a question?"

"Sure."

"Was this just about the story?"

Joanie is silent for a moment, gathering her answer. "No Aeron. I am just a conduit. I did not betray Sara or you. I am doing my job for someone I care deeply about. My admiration for Sara will be felt in these stories.

I will not rest until that son of a bitch and every person around him is in jail. You can bet on that."

I look over at her, and she glances at me. I look back out in the wilderness, "I believe you, Joanie."

"Thanks, Aeron." She reaches over and squeezes my hand.

We arrived back at the motel. She asks if I need anything, and I decline. I stepped out of the SUV, and she let me know the story will be in the morning edition of the post and will probably be picked up by every major newspaper and cable news network by mid-morning. She expresses that I need to prepare for the incoming flood of media that is going to want statements and interviews from me. I am still in a state where I cannot comprehend any of that. I am just exhausted, numb, dead on the inside. I asked her to contact me in the morning and maybe be in a better place to deal with the avalanche coming. I slowly walked back to the room. As I enter, I can smell Sara's presence, maybe subconsciously, I don't know. I fall on the bed, the adrenaline drains and I am out in a matter of minutes.

Chapter 46

My phone starts to go off a little after 6:00 am. All my old morning opening managers have texted me with pretty much the same message, "What the hell is going on? Are you watching the news?" I turn the local TV on. Nothing yet. Savannah is the closest big city, and the Berlin events have no impact on them. The ramifications of what will happen today are starting to blanket me as I immediately jump in the shower. My phone is ready to get quite a workout.

More texts and calls ramp up after 7:00 am. Tom Bridges needs to talk to me. Joanie checks in to see if I am okay and if I have a copy of the post yet. Jeff Peeples, Tom Timlin, and Mary Fogle want to get on the phone ASAP. My priority is coffee, and I head to the hotel office. As I walk in, the clerk, white as a sheet, watches the Good Morning America lead story Alleged Cult Raid in Georgia. A picture from my Facebook account appears on the screen, and I would have picked a better one. Sara, Dan, the "intern," "hamster," and others appear at various times during the three-plus minute story. GMA reporter Whit Johnson is on location at the compound discussing the 'explosive and hard to believe story of murder, conspiracy, and religion.' I am still standing in the doorway when the story ends. I ask the clerk, "Coffee Fresh?" he responds, "Uhhh, Yeah, in the machine." I try to be as normal as I can in that situation. Head down, get the coffee, and leave. Walk back to the room; the coffee is still like tar. I take a big breath, start the checklist of calls that I need to make, and bear down...

One week later, I arrived at Tallahassee International Airport for Sara's funeral. I flew in from Savannah. I spent the week there dealing with the FBI, GBI, and all the reporters and television people looking to capitalize on the biggest story of the year. I spoke to Joanie before I got on the plane. They are already talking about Pulitzer with her reporting on the events in Berlin. Her headline on that first Friday morning was "Sex Cult Business Leader Taken Down By 'Feminine' Hero." I wonder if she came up with that one herself. A series of stories throughout the week exposed Dan Rand for what he is and was. Sara did an amazing job of compiling the evidence necessary for the story. Joanie gave me a shout-out for some of my research. She assured me that state and local charges are pending, and Dan may never see the light of day again. Murder, conspiracy, fraud, blackmail. No bond for those types of charges. Ali Howard and Laura Staley may get the worst of all of it. The "intern" is looking at Murder 1 for Sophie, Kim, and Sara, the "hamster" accessory and conspiracy to commit murder. Comptor was seized by the Feds on Monday and will more than likely be dissolved. The hundreds of employees or maybe victims will have a long haul being deprogrammed from this nightmare they were caught up in. Victims come in all shapes in this type of situation. I saw it all over the news this week. The damage a cult can do is something I never understood until several weeks ago. The ultimate betrayal of trust, commitment, hope, love. We all lost that in some way. What I lost came down to just one person, Sara. I have had her swimming in my head all week. No dreams, nightmares, just thoughts. She made the ultimate sacrifice for the good of the world. I think no one will truly appreciate that as much as I do. The power and impact of just one person to make things right is the lesson I learned above all others.

The funeral will be on Saturday, a little over seven days since she left this world. I am still not alright or even okay with anything about it. I arrived on Friday morning, but have not had a chance to process her to the fullest of being gone. Her parents were kind enough to allow me to stay with them. Sara had told them all about me even before she connected the first time. I got in an Uber and headed from the airport. We have a viewing that night, and it will be the first time I will have seen her since saying goodbye at the compound. I cannot talk to anyone about how I feel about her. It is insane even for me to think about. I just wish I could thank her for saving me. I wish I had the opportunity to love her, even if I would always be second to Sam. With a woman like Sara, being second still isn't a bad place to be. I see the streets roll by in the Uber, going in and out of reflections. Past life, present life, future life. Having a different perspective on it all is the gift Sara gave me. I have a responsibility to do right by her going forward. I arrived at Sara's parents Rob and Olivia's home. They greet me on the porch. Olivia has Sara's smile and Rob's eyes. I feel her presence all around me. They showed me to the room and told me we had to leave in a few hours for the viewing. I lie in bed and close my eyes for a bit. I do not know how to feel about seeing Sara in a casket. I need to be strong, silent, and supportive. That is what she would do.

Rob and Olivia are nice enough to drive to the funeral home for the viewing. I purchased a suit while still in Savannah. Navy Blue, not custom, a white shirt, striped blue, and black tie. I would make a great insurance agent. I get out of the car and get myself right, straighten the tie, tuck the shirt deeper into my pants, and one button on the jacket. I wanted to look good for her. In some crazy way, I think she will be watching all of us tonight. I refrain from going in right away. Rob and Olivia know what they need to do, so I stay outside. Reside in the parking lot and pace for a while. Guests start to arrive. I know none of them until I see Joanie Woodward. She is wearing a beautiful red dress that accentuates all the best in her tall, lean frame. She is wearing sunglasses and has a stern look on her face.

"Hi Aeron, get inside. The reporters are coming."

"Reporters, at a viewing?"

"They are looking for you, parents, anyone who is willing to talk. Is there security?"

"I have no idea."

"Let's just get inside. It should be fine until we are ready to leave."

"Nice to see you, Joanie," I smile.

"Good to see you too, Aeron."

"Your stories this week are pretty amazing. You did this whole thing justice."

"Thanks, a lot to comb through. This Dan Rand was quite a piece."

"Sara seemed to be ahead of all of this."

"That and then some. What this guy was planning to do is frightening. When I was looking through Sara's notes, I found a line in the margins of her notebook... She referred to Hitler a few times."

"Hitler? Where would she get that from?"

"I don't know exactly, but I think she looked at how warped he was with his theories and his pure hatred and insecurity about men, especially in business. It is like she found some sort of parallel with the Jews. He just wanted to destroy anything male. Pretty sick. Again, I may be projecting, but from her notes, it was a conclusion she kept coming to."

"Sara was so determined to stop him. I would not be stunned if she took whatever the theory was and had to change history. I wish I had that type of forethought."

"I will tell you, Aeron, she was smart enough to get both of us involved. I think she needed the right people to help put the pieces together. She was a hell of a leader."

"Yeah, it is a shame she won't be able to carry on with that."

"I know, I am sorry. You became quite fond of her."

"More than fond, Joanie."

She pauses and snaps us out of the conversation, "Let's go in. We need to pay our respects."

Joanie puts her arm in mine and makes our way into the funeral parlor. People are mingling in the foyer; we walk by and head into the viewing room. The casket is open, and I ask Joanie to go ahead. I need to stand back for a bit before I make the approach to see her one last time. I watch Joanie walk up to the casket. Rob and Olivia greet her with a hug, and tears start to flow. Her sisters Stacy and Sophia both have the same sensibility as Sara as they embrace the visitors. Such a beautiful family. I tilted my head back, knowing that my turn was coming. I put my head in my hands, took a breath, and got up out of the folded chair. I make my way to the aisle and to the casket. Olivia grabs me and holds me tight. Sara must have said some really good things about me that I do not know about. Rob shook my hand and grabbed my shoulder. I thanked them both and moved a few feet to the casket. The sisters embraced me and let me have my moment. I look down at first, then transfer my gaze to Sara in her resting place. I take her all in at once. She is dressed in a long blue and white dress with gray flat shoes and stockings. She is wearing a cross necklace and diamond earrings. It is the kind of outfit I could see her answering the door for me when I would come to pick her up to take her out for a night on the town. Her face looks so peaceful. I wish I could see her eyes. She has just the right amount of makeup to bring out the best in her cheekbones and lips. She is beautiful and will always be beautiful. She exudes the best in humanity, and it is there in her casket. I just stared at her. Her right hand is over her left, sitting on her diaphragm. I placed my hand on top and looked at her face, hoping her eyes would open. I close mine and say a prayer I know will be unanswered. I open my eyes and she is still in the same place. I think to kiss her on the cheek and then think the best of it to not. I lightly squeeze her hand and just mouth, "Thank you." I hope no one noticed that. I turn and walk back to the foyer. I continue to the restroom, I need a stall to have my meltdown. I sit on the commode and cry for what feels like an eternity, but is only a few minutes. I feel my breathing start to stabilize again, and walk out of the stall, splash water on my face, and meet with Rob and Olivia. This is just the start. The funeral is in the morning. One last goodbye to sweet Sara.

Chapter 47

Rob and Olivia set up a reception at the Lincoln Center in Tallahassee. The capacity of 250 is exceeded, with so many wanting to pay respects and celebrate the life of Sara O'Connor. I had a drink for the first time in over three weeks. I have more than a few. I just sit and watch as people hug, talk, laugh, and share memories of an incredible life that I wish I had known more of. Joanie checks in on me a few times, but she has her hands full dealing with friends and reporters, trying to get comments from anyone who wants to talk about Sara or the story. It is funny that Joanie is as much the story now as she is covering it. I get to a point where I have had enough and ask Rob if I could just go home on my own. He hugged me, gave me the house key, and I Uber back to their place. I walk into the empty house and open the fridge. A few beers on the back of the fourth shelf. I take the best option, An Amstel light and just take my time perusing through the house. I see pictures of Sara, Sam and Sam Jr. on the mantle in the living room. The sisters together. A hallway full of a retrospective from childhood, vacations, graduation and adulthood. They were such proud parents. I find what her room was. I open to see the bed she probably slept in, trophies on an antique dresser from high school and college. I look down at the floor, feeling ashamed that I am so noisy and head to my room. I get ready for bed, but I still have half a beer to finish. I lay back on the headboard, cross-legged beer in my lap, and just continued to try and come to terms. No answers will come tonight. I down the last quarter of the beer, turn off the light and try to get to sleep.

I open my eyes in a field of white lilies. Look around and get my bearings. The sun is so bright, yet beautiful and warm. I do not have any fear, just curiosity. I do not want to wake up from this dream, but I do not know where I am. I stand, stretch, and see in the distance three figures. Two adults and one much smaller, maybe a child. I start to walk to them; the wind feels good on my face. I am not wearing shoes; the freedom feels so nice. As I got closer, the three noticed me. One whispers in the other ears, and the person breaks away. I do not know if it is a woman or a man. We started to walk toward each other. The brightness covers the face of the person coming toward me. It gets brighter the closer I get. I squint and almost have to close my eyes completely. It is so bright, then the voice. The light disappears. It is Sara. "Aeron," she grabs my hands. "Sara, I miss you so much." "Aeron, I will always be with you. You never have to miss me. I am home now, and it is time for you to go home. You have so much to do. So many need you now. You have no idea." "Sara, I don't know what you mean. No one needs me. I am alone." "You are wrong, Aeron." She smiles that sweet Sara smile, "You have so much to do. I am so excited to watch what the world will be like when you realize how special you are." "But Sara, I don't understand." "Trust me, Aeron, I am with you. I need to get back to my Sambies, but never ever forget that I am always with you. We came together to do so much to better the world. My part is done. It is time for you to finish the job." She touches my

*cheek, and I grab her hand to shed a tear. I still do not com-
prehend what she wants from me, but I need to trust her.
The betrayal of life is over. I need to understand that and
embrace the future. Still have so much to do. She steps away,
and I watch her dissolve in front of me. I know I am in a
dream, but also know that will be the last I see of her. Sara
has given me my purpose. It is up to me now to fulfill what
that is.*

I wake up with the sun shining through the room.
I start to cry, not as much for loss, but for love. I will say
my final farewell to Sara today with everyone who loved
her. That is an incredible gift that has been put upon me.

The funeral is my last chance to take the spirit before being put to rest. I spend most of the time at the
gravesite, just trying not to be in the way. Rob and Olivia
are dueling roles as grieving parents and hosts. The sisters
are there to comfort all comers. They do an amazing job
at balancing both. I do not know how they can do it. The
more I watch them, the more I see where Sara got her
sensibilities from. These are all such good people. She
came from good stock.

The priest gives a beautiful yet antiseptic tribute
at the grave. I am being harsh, but am sensitive to Sara
and placing her on a pedestal. I wanted to speak, but who
was I? A few weeks ago, no one here even knew me. I did
not even save her life. If I did, we would not be here now.
I think of her in my dream from the night before. So glad
I am wearing sunglasses. My eyes are of no use to anyone
today. I wish I had just felt sadness. I don't. My anger,
confusion, and helplessness creep in as I sit in a chair just
feet from her casket. Now is not the time to analyze all of
that. Many nights alone in my living room will be sufficient. The service ends, and the group of 30-40 disperse

back to their cars. The last lunch reception is to have a few more drinks, stories, and memories and to go back to the real world. Rob and Olivia are nice enough to ask if I want to stay with them for a while. I decline long term but would like a few more days to be in this presence before I must force what the new reality will be. As I settle for the night, my phone goes off. I look, and my breath is taken away. It is Alec.

Chapter 48

I stare at his name on the phone; I do not even want to look at the message. I decided to leave it until morning. I am glad I did. Olivia brings me a nightcap and sits on the bed with me as we both drink a strong bourbon and soda. We talk; she is the essence of a mother, and I enjoy the calming relief of her in the room with me. She is not that much older than me, but I feel so childlike in her company. Again, I can feel Sara, and that is comforting now on the day she was laid to rest.

I sleep well, no dreams or nightmares. I wake at ease, grab the phone, and know I need to look, possibly respond to the man who, without knowing, has put me in this place. I saw a group text from Jeff and Tom. I chose to take them first. "Can we talk today? We need you, bud." There is the 'need' word again. I responded, and we planned a call in an hour. I leave Alec alone until after this is done. I go out for coffee and find a little café that is a good place to take a call. After a strong double espresso, I took the call from Jeff and Tom.

"Hey guys, how are you doing?" I feel good to have them both on the phone with me.

"Good, Aeron." They both say in kind. Jeff starts the chat, "You are a celebrity in town here now, bud. Cannot believe all the stories we have heard about Dan and all that... Look, Bob Willogos wants to talk to you. He is terminating all contracts with Comptor for cause, and they need someone to take over everything. He wants us to do it, but honestly, we need help. Are you coming back?"

I take the statement in, knowing where 'need' comes from now. Maybe I do have some worth through the need. "Yeah, Jeff, I am coming home in a few days. I am more than happy to help with what they want."

"That would be great. Tom and I started an LLC, and we need some heavy consulting. All the contracts are up for grabs now, and I think we are in a great position. Just need some help getting all the important stuff you are good at taken care of."

"Sure, Jeff. I know once you guys get things going, it will be fine. Can I ask... Has Alec tried to get a hold of you?"

"Yep...After Dan was arrested. I am ignoring all his calls. Fuck him."

"Good, that is probably the right decision."

"He actually wants to help. He reached out to Bob. He told him thanks, but no thanks. What a scumbag."

"I will be back in town on Wednesday. Why don't you set up a meeting with Bob on Thursday? We will get together on Wednesday afternoon. There is a lot you two need to know about the contracts and nuances. Your mindset will need to change as you transition to business owners, K."

"I know, Aeron, we are ready. Appreciate you so much helping us out here. We know we can do this."

"I know you both can, too. We will figure it all out."

They both thanked me in unison. I hang up and smile. I have a reason to go back home now. I take a breath and know I have to finally look at Alec's text. I do, simply, "Can we talk?" I know I can't put this off any longer. "Sure, Alec. What's on your mind?" He surprises me by responding almost immediately. "I am in Tallahassee. Can we meet today?" I am stunned and surprised. The autopilot kicks in. "Yes, let's meet. What time?" "How about 6:00, The Black Horseradish on Monroe? I will make reservations." I shake my head and respond, "Okay, Alec, I will see you then." "Great, looking forward to it, bud." He used "bud" with me after everything. I sighed and put the phone down. Take in the sunlight from the outdoor seat at the café. It is quite peaceful and will give me plenty of time to think before meeting the man who changed everything for me.

I make my way back to the house. I don't speak about the meeting with Alec. Rob and Olivia continue to be wonderful hosts. I feel that they have grown fond of me. Maybe they are just not ready to deal with what a new normal without Sara will look like. When I think about these wonderful people who have lost a daughter, a son-in-law, and a grandson, I become overwhelmed with how they can go on. The grief and the pain must be so monumental. How does some semblance of betrayal not creep into both of their thoughts? The face they put on is so brave, lovely and everything I saw in their daughter. I do not have to tell them. They know, I think they know that I know. That is consolation for them. I go to my room to prepare for the meeting with Alec. I turn my thoughts to this man who was my daily companion for 20 years, and I feel like I never knew him. Preparation is fruitless. I am determined to go into this meeting with the lessons

I learned over the last several weeks, and I believe that I have the power. I take a long shower and think about Alec. His face, body language, vocal tone, bullshit. I am not one to be an alpha dog, but that may be the direction I need to go. To be honest, I have no idea how I will be. The man in my head never solidifies in the real world. Always been the trouble I have had. I think that I may have someone looking out for me this time, like no one else in my life before. I will hold Sara close to me and be confident her presence and bravery will help to push me toward the desired result. I call an Uber, dress, and head out to the Black Horseradish.

The trip to the restaurant is about ten minutes, not much time to think, which is probably a good thing. I get let out front and head into the bar area. I see Alec in the center of the bar, talking to the bartender and another guest to his right. He is wearing blue slacks, a green polo shirt, boat shoes, no socks. I have seen this outfit many times before. I walk up, and he looks so happy to see me. Obviously, has had a few drinks before my arrival. "Hey, here is my right-hand man, Aeron. These folks are Joe, the bartender, and Sam, who is from Miami, a Big Dolphin's fan. I told him about the entire starting offensive line in Super Bowl 7. He didn't know that." Alec is always so proud of his worthless sports knowledge. "You wanna sit here, bud?" "No, Alec, let's get a table." He responds, a bit miffed, "Okay."

We got a table in the back of the restaurant. This is a weeknight; the place is not too busy. I am happy for less distractions. Keep focused on what is to come.

"This is a great place; I have been here a few times. Excellent beer selection. You know I love good beer. Wanna try this IPA I am drinking?" He is in a very good mood and comfortable.

"I am fine, Alec. When did you get to town? Why are you in town?"

"I knew you were here. The newspapers and TV have been talking about this for days now. I know you did a couple of pressers here, and you are staying with Sara O'Connor's parents. She was a nice girl."

"Yes, she was. Pretty remarkable, really."

"A shame with all that happened. You know, I knew Dan was strange with the whole religious thing, but never imagined he was that crazy."

I am getting a little irritated in just the first couple minutes, "Alec, what do you want?"

He pauses, and I know this look. The salesman hat is about to go on, "Well, I should just cut to it. I know all of Dan's company holdings have either been seized, or the client contracts have been voided. This is a great opportunity. I have been trying to connect with Jeff and Tom. I know that Liberty wants to work with them, but they can't do it alone. Not ready for any of that. We can move in and show the strength to be able to reacquire those accounts and the rest, too."

"So, you want to undercut Jeff and Tom?"

"No, I want to work with them, but if they do not want to team up here, we have the history, and we can do it."

"We?"

"Yes, we. What do you think? We did this for years. These clients are going to be scooped up by someone."

"Why not it be us, Alec, right?"

"Exactly. I figure we can go in and do the consulting first and lay the foundation, then close. You can get the research done for where each one is at right now, and we can even take on a bunch of the other Comptor accounts along with the original Vivant's."

"Sounds like you have it all figured out. Maybe you can create some 'client experience manager' position for me or someone else while you are at it."

"That's a great idea, Aeron. When do you want to get started?"

"Alec, can I ask you a question?"

"Shoot."

"Does Barb know?"

"About?"

"Kyra."

"Why would you ask me that?"

"I saw the video, Alec. That's why Sara found me."

"I talked to the FBI, and my wife knows what she needs to know."

"So, she doesn't know about the affair."

"Barb knows what she needs to know. That is it."

"You lost your company; I lost my career, and Sara lost her life because you were manipulated by Dan and his team. Your wife doesn't know anything, and now you just want things to be how they were before. Does that sound about right?"

"Look, Aeron. We don't have to hurt more people. I made some big mistakes, but we can make it right now. I want to make it up to you."

"By stabbing Jeff and Tom in the back while you are at it?"

"Are you going to hold a grudge like this, when I am talking about a huge opportunity to get everything back?"

The tension at the table is starting to rise, and I am ready to throw my grenade. "Alec, you betrayed us. I told you that back in November. I was on the verge of suicide about three weeks ago, and this woman came to me and saved my life. She is not going to die in vain."

"Are you working on some kind of threat, Aeron?"

"I am sure you have read Joanie Woodward's reporting on all of this, right?"

"Yes, pretty thorough stuff."

"I have spoken to her sparingly. You do know she went to college with Sara, and we were friends for years?"

"I did not."

"She told me I could call her anytime if I had additional information or wanted to do an exclusive sit down. That video and the Kyra Bacon situation seem like a really great story, don't you?"

He stares menacingly at me. I had never seen that look before but knew I had him. "What do you want, Aeron?"

I just stare at him; I want to relish this moment for a moment. "Two things. Back out of all business dealings with current and former clients. Tell your wife about the affair."

"You're nuts, no fucking way."

"I have her number pulled up on my phone, wanna see? All I need to do is push send. Hell, we can both talk to her if you like."

He sits intently for a minute. I put my hands on my lap. I am willing as long as it takes for a response.

"Okay, I will back out of the business stuff. I will let Jeff and Tom take it all on."

"And your wife?"

"Can I think about that for a few days?"

"Sure, you can get back to me. Oh, by the way, I am meeting with Jeff and Tom later this week. They want me to be a consultant for them and the clients. First meeting is with Bob Willogos at Tidal this week."

The color drains from his face. He knows he is cooked. "I guess we are done."

"Yeah, I think we are done here, Alec."

"I will get the..."

"Don't worry about it. I will get your tab. Go home, Alec, and lose my number, please."

He slowly gets up and walks toward the door. I am seeing for the last time a man who gave me everything and took it all away. I don't know if I will ever completely get over the betrayal, but I have found a sliver of redemption in the last thirty minutes. As he leaves, I take a deep breath, gather myself, pay the tab, and leave. I need to get back and pack for home.

Chapter 49

I get back to Rob and Olivia's and let them know I am leaving in a few days. I make reservations to head back home, and I spend a few more nights wanting to learn anything I can about Sara and her life. They are accommodating at every turn. I see photo albums, awards, and school items. They offer me a few things of hers. They can see how much I care about her. I accept a cross necklace that was given to her by Rob on her wedding day. It is beautiful and simple. I know there is a part of her in it. I thanked them, and they offered to take me to the airport. I decline. They have done enough for me. They now need time to repair the pain and try to move on. In so many ways, so do I.

I wake up the next morning, and the flight leaves at 10:30 am. I should be home before 1:00 pm. My phone went off. It is Jeff. "Still picking you up at the airport, K." "Sounds good, bud." "Tom will be with me; we want to start talking right away this afternoon." "Okay, I will be ready." "Aeron, we are so excited to have you back. This is going to be awesome." "Great, Jeff, see you at 1," I say goodbye to these wonderful people who have cared for me since the death of their daughter. They offer an open invite to come down anytime. I would take them up on that every week if I could, but with my nature, I feel I may never see them again. Hate to impose. Never feel welcome. It is my own head, not theirs. I got in the car and headed out. As the car travels, so do my thoughts about what has transpired since that email came across my computer: I Need You. I have figured out that I do have more worth and power than I believed. I discovered love in a completely unique way than I ever imagined. I have a purpose again, maybe even a future. That comes with more pain, yet that is life. We gain, we lose, we adapt, we move on. The car arrives at the airport. I grabbed my bag and headed into the terminal. Check-in and make my way to the gate. As I walk, I faintly hear a familiar song but cannot quite make it out. As I travel under a speaker, I stop in my tracks. It plays above me, "Sara...Sara...No time is a good time for goodbye..." I whisper, "Isn't that right, Sara?" I smile. It is time to move forward.

The End